Object Relations in Depression

This book examines the role of British object relations theory in order to explore our understanding and treatment of depression. It challenges current conceptualizations of depression while simultaneously discussing the complex nature of depression, its long-lasting and chronic implications and the susceptibility to relapse many may face.

Illuminated throughout by case studies, areas of discussion include:

- Freud's theory of depression
- analytic subtypes of depression
- a theoretical contribution to the problem of relapse
- the correlation between dream work and the work of mourning.

Object Relations in Depression offers a psychoanalytic discussion of the multifaceted nature of depression and as such will be of great interest to all those in the psychoanalytic field.

Trevor Lubbe trained as a child psychotherapist at the Tavistock Clinic and worked in the NHS before returning to South Africa, where he now lives and works. He is a member of the Association of Child Psychotherapists and a member of the Institute for Child Psychoanalytic Psychotherapy in South Africa.

Object Relations in Depression

A return to theory

Trevor Lubbe

Routledge
Taylor & Francis Group

LONDON AND NEW YORK

First published 2011 by Routledge
27 Church Road, Hove, East Sussex BN3 2FA

Simultaneously published in the USA and Canada
by Routledge
270 Madison Avenue, New York, NY 10016

Routledge is an imprint of the Taylor & Francis Group, an Informa business

Typeset in Times by Garfield Morgan, Swansea, West Glamorgan
Printed and bound in Great Britain by TJ International Ltd, Padstow,
Cornwall
Paperback cover design by Andrew Ward

This publication has been produced with paper manufactured to strict
environmental standards and with pulp derived from sustainable forests.

British Library Cataloguing in Publication Data
A catalogue record for this book is available from the British Library

Library of Congress Cataloging-in-Publication Data
Lubbe, Trevor, 1952-
    Object relations in depression : a return to theory / Trevor Lubbe.
        p. ; cm.
    ISBN 978-0-415-57676-5 (hbk) – ISBN 978-0-415-57677-2 (pbk.)
1. Depression, Mental. 2. Object relations (Psychoanalysis) I. Title.
    [DNLM: 1. Depressive Disorder. 2. Object Attachment. 3. Psychoanalytic
Theory. WM 171]
    RC537.L75 2010
    616.85'27–dc22

                                                                    2010030714

ISBN: 978-0-415-57676-5 (hbk)
ISBN: 978-0-415-57677-2 (pbk)

The outer is the object of our observation but not of our interest. Thus the fisherman sits and directs attention unwaveringly on the float, yet the float does not interest him, only the movements down on the seabed.

Søren Kierkegaard (1843)

When theories don't work, don't check the facts, read the theory again.

Russian saying

Contents

Preface

This is an account, written by a young woman in her mid-twenties, describing, in retrospect, her experience of subsiding into depression.

It all started with feeling bored, then feeling bored and glum, then feeling bored, glum and tired, then bored, glum, tired and anxious. Then the sighing started. Sighing in the bath; sighing in the lift; sighing at the disco. Then coming home and seeing all those dishes in the sink and thinking, 'I'll get those later' – only to find them still sitting there several days later. Then one morning I woke up in terror and not knowing what it was – I could not breathe, I could not swallow – was I having a heart attack? Then, the first consultation with my GP. Everything shipshape – liver, heart, blood pressure, bowel, no sign of infection. By the 4th week, however, everyday life had become a massive, meaningless effort. Did I eat this morning? Was I really hungry? Does it make any difference? Look at that melon in the fridge. I'll have to find a plate to put it on; I'll have to cut it up into pieces; I'll have to chew it; Oh God, then I'll have to swallow it. By the late afternoon you feel sad and sorry for yourself. Then you cry and feel totally helpless. Negative thoughts keep coming up and they spread and spread. Don't feel like going to a movie. Don't feel like going to the gym. Have to get ready for the party; don't feel well; don't know what to wear. I feel ugly; I look terrible. Two hours later you decide to stay at home and watch 'Survivor'. I couldn't believe this was happening to me – I was so jittery all the time! But then you notice the numbing set in, feeling a little less, and little less, and a little less each day. People say you're just down, you'll feel better tomorrow but every tomorrow is a *Groundhog Day* – the panic when waking up at 3 a.m.; the total silence outside in the world as you make a cup the tea; the pretending everything is fine at work when it's not; the pretending everything is fine with friends when it's not; the pretending everything is fine with mum and dad when it's not. Then by the afternoon you feel better but you dread going home. You'd rather do anything than go home because at home you have to face horrible thoughts of what's wrong with you. I couldn't go on! Depression was not my friend! But in true *Groundhog* fashion you go to bed thinking that after a good night's sleep you'll wake up the next morning feeling that it would have all gone away. But you wake up at 3 a.m. with that sickening feeling and you watch the world falling to pieces on CNN.

Acknowledgements

The inspiration for this book came from two sources. First, from the Eighth International Neuro-Psychoanalysis Congress held in Vienna in July 2007, which brought together experts in neurobiology, neuroanatomy, pharmacology, clinical psychology and psychoanalysis to wrestle with the subject of depression in the context of contemporary interdisciplinary thinking. This was a fascinating convergence of ideas that led to a great deal of mutual learning and cross-fertilization, and I am indebted to Professor Mark Solms for his opening address on 'Psychoanalytic Approaches to Depression' that, with permission, I have employed in Chapter 2 as a springboard for setting down the theoretical foundations of this book. Second, as a clinician I was drawn to the area of a notorious miasma surrounding the use of SSRIs (selective serotonin reuptake inhibitors) for treating juvenile depression by the indiscriminate prescription practices of child psychiatrists and general practitioners (GPs) in the Greater Johannesburg area of South Africa. The result is a polemic (Chapter 12) that challenges the rationale and the rationality of these practices given the questionable research findings on the safety and efficacy of antidepressants for children.

To get my bearings on the specialist aspect of this book, I tried out some chapters in a series of lectures and seminars to the Johannesburg Association of Child Psychotherapy and to the Cape Town Society of Psychoanalytic Psychotherapy, and I offer my thanks to them for the comments and reservations I received. To a small number of friends and colleagues I owe not only thanks for their support but also an apology for my absences and inattentiveness during the time it took to incubate, prepare and complete this book. As Spike Milligan once said, you find out who your friends are when you are trying to be creative with, and in, depression. Thank you Jenny, Eric, Judy, and Stu, and a special appreciation to Frances Williams for her editorial clarity and her invaluable suggestions in reading the manuscript as a whole. I must also without reservation express my indebtedness to a group of patients who over the years taught me great humility and patience in understanding their grim and often flickering struggle with depression and its effects on their loved ones. Finally, I would like to dedicate this book to the memory of my parents, whom I came to know all too briefly but who nonetheless carry on being constant companions to me when meeting the next eventful turn in the road.

A further acknowledgement must be made to Dr Hugo Bleichmar and the *International Journal of Psychoanalysis* for permission to publish his diagram depicting the pathways leading to different subtypes of depression. Similarly, I am grateful to Random House Inc. for permission to use an excerpt from 'Lull', a poem by Theodore Roethke.

Finally, it has been a great pleasure to work again with Kate Hawes and Sarah Gibson and their team at Psychology Press and Routledge Mental Health (Taylor & Francis Group) who were supportive throughout. Thanks must also go to the advisory reporters for their comments that were both helpful and trenchant when it came to challenging the shibboleths regarding present-day popular and popularized treatments of depression.

Chapter 1

Depression today

A critical point in understanding and treatment

Introduction

Depression is distinguished by feeling ill. This sense of illness is characterized by inner moods of feeling despondent for most of the day, tiredness, tearfulness, loss of interest in usually pleasurable activities, and feeling that nothing matters. These moods are usually brought on by inner body panic and other physical disturbances of sleep, activity, appetite and digestion that then go on to fill out the conventional clinical picture. Apart from these inner disruptions the sights and sounds of the outside world too can feel like an assault. So depression is an illness of severance – one's normal contact with the inner and outer life is severed.

Many people feel ill in this way without necessarily suffering a personal loss or tragedy. So each depression, as with each anxiety, has a hidden pattern that calls out to be understood from the point of view of individual meaning. This is essentially the psychoanalytic attitude towards depression.

Since the late 1980s, the successful treatment of depression has been bedevilled by two pincer-like movements that have ultimately joined forces to create one of the biggest challenges for researchers, service providers and clinicians working in this area. Following the discovery of a new class of antidepressants tested in tandem with standardized short-term psychological therapies, there was widespread optimism and conviction that the treatment of depression would be revolutionized. Unfortunately, the gloomy news today is that as depression is set to become the second largest cause of global disability (World Health Organization (WHO) 2001), current treatment pathways for depression have shown little sign of achieving more than 50 per cent success in remission rates.

A first response has been to concede the true complexity of depression and to identify with more clarity its most pernicious clinical feature – chronicity and its vulnerability to relapse. For this purpose the old acronym 'TRD' – treatment resistant depression – was revived for patients for whom two courses of antidepressants had not worked. Previously TRD was treated with electric therapy. What has been more difficult to digest is the uncomfortable reality that mainstream treatment modalities have failed the patient population and possibly aggravated the problem of relapse.

The predicaments in treating depression successfully have been flagged for some time, culminating in two important reviews of treatment outcome research (Corvelyn et al. 2005; Roth and Fonagy 2006). In their review Roth and Fonagy (2006) confirmed that in depressed patients who were offered 'treatment as usual'[1] – 79 per cent with mild depression (dysthymic disorder) were likely to develop severe depression (major depressive disorder: MDD). In the case of dysthymics with a superimposed MDD (double depression) clinical outcomes were worse. Even among those dysthymics who responded to treatment, especially antidepressant treatment alone, residual symptoms persisted and were associated with an increased likelihood of relapse. In other words, with antidepressant monotherapy their condition became mild but chronic.

It should be clear how imperative effective treatment is for dysthymics if they are not to swell the statistics for major depressive disorder. However, MDD is already the leading cause of disability in the United States for the age group 15–44. Indeed, the outlook is bleak: 85 per cent of patients with MDD followed up over fifteen years, and 75 per cent of patients followed up over ten years will have suffered a relapse (Roth and Fonagy 2006, p. 103).

In their own review Corvelyn et al. (2005) add that compared to a placebo response of 30–35 per cent positive outcomes for antidepressant therapy have achieved only 50 per cent effectiveness. Moreover, when unpublished studies are incorporated they report that drug/placebo differences reach levels of questionable clinical significance. While there is good evidence that long-term treatment with antidepressants can stave off relapse, there is no correlation between the length of drug treatment and the likelihood of relapse once medication is discontinued. In other words, it does not matter whether you treat a depressed patient for three months or three years if medication is stopped relapse is certain – in fact, the risk of relapse is significantly greater after longer treatment (Fava 2002). In the main, this review anticipates the tide of scepticism that currently exists regarding the benefits of SSRIs statistically relative to inert substances.

In addition to evaluating the record of pharmacological treatment, Corvelyn et al. (2005) provide an assessment of the uneven results from short-term treatments such as cognitive-behavioural therapy (CBT), interpersonal therapy (IPT) or brief dynamic psychotherapy (BDP). The results, in fact, mimic those for pharmacological treatments: in around 50 per cent of patients in trials there are good rates of remission of symptoms (especially in mild depression), but at one year of follow-up 50 per cent of those who recovered will suffer a relapse. The authors refer to the famous and oft-quoted study – the US National Institute of Mental Health (NIMH) Treatment of Depression Collaborative Research Program (summarized in

Elkin 1994) – that at the time was a cautionary lesson for the many advocates of short-term treatments. This study subsequently received a number of subsidiary or meta-analyses, but the general conclusion was that while structured therapies in brief formats (duration of sixteen weeks) show clear benefit (no advantage to any treatment method) these interventions are insufficient in sustaining functioning in the majority of patients. To remedy this situation 'booster' or 'maintenance' therapy have been recommended as the best safeguard in warding off relapse (Roth and Fonagy 2006).[2]

What are we to conclude from these dismal findings – that depression is a mood disorder with no cure? Or, that once you develop depression, it becomes an unremitting problem that merely metamorphosizes from one thing into another? Roth and Fonagy (2006) seem to imply that relapse is intrinsic to clinical course, and that at best treatments can bring about only temporary remission. In that case, critical questions should surely be posed about the value of mainstream treatments. What role have they played in the burgeoning incidence of so-called treatment-resistant depression? In reading between the lines of these two reviews, it is difficult not to form the impression that customary treatment regimes have made little impact on a core aspect of the morphology of depression – which leads to the suspicion that an important structural factor in depression has been woefully ignored or, historically, underestimated.

This situation has come about notwithstanding the development of a seminal system for the use by researchers and clinicians in the form of the DSM-IV – which, on paper, provided the ideal operational tool for establishing empirical competence in three crucial areas: testing the validity and reliability of diagnostic criteria; developing theories of psychopathology; and generating vast empires of clinical research on every aspect of any designated disorder. Nevertheless, in spite of this tool many clinicians working with depression nowadays are still unsure whether the distinction between MDD and dysthymic disorder is reliable, not to mention the difficulties encountered in bracketing the variations within MDD (McCullough et al. 2000). Furthermore, Westen et al. (2002) point to the persistence of two nagging problems with the DSM classification of mood disorders – the issues of sub-threshold symptoms and comorbidity.

Therefore, while offering many obvious advantages the current diagnostic system with its atheoretical nosological approach has left us unexpectedly less secure in our knowledge about depression, and less confident in the relationship between research and practice. Hence, it is not surprising that in both reviews, sharing these concerns, the authors carry exhortations for continued research in three key areas in their conclusions.

What they recommend in common are first, conceptualizing depression within a developmental or lifespan framework, that is, in the context of normal development; second, giving more weight to characterological or personality variables; third, addressing the problem of the recurrence and chronicity. The implication in these recommendations is that depression as an illness must take into account the depressed individual.

To my way of thinking these recommendations suggest a pressing need to return to theory in order to make better sense of these gloomy research findings, both on the natural history of depression and its apparent refractory nature. I believe a return to both past as well as to contemporary psychoanalytic theories on depression may be especially relevant to all the recommendations mentioned above. Theory has a deep heuristic value for the clinician. It opens up access to the imagination of the clinician when there are puzzling or worrying data that appear to defy understanding. Moreover, not only may new ideas emerge, but also embedded aspects of existing (or past) theory may be rediscovered. Hence, one important intention of this book is to demonstrate how a particular strand of thinking within psychoanalytic theory – British object relations theory – may permit a different conceptualization of the structure of depression that, in turn, may allow some alternative thoughts to be brought to bear on the apparent intractability of the disorder, as well on the thorny problem of relapse. This project therefore should rightly begin with a brief commentary of the above recommendations with the purpose of adding a contribution from the point of view of psychoanalytic theory.

Developmental framework

First, what may be particularly useful to the research community is a basic theoretical assumption in psychoanalytic theory that depression, like anxiety, is a fundamental affect that is a natural psychobiological occurrence and a living byproduct of the stages of infantile and adolescent development. Within these stages there are maturational processes and tasks that precipitate psychological states of anxiety and conflict to which depression is frequently a healthy response. Where this response diverges from the norm, this implies that certain conflicts and defences have come to the fore that have compromised the successful negotiation of these developmental undertakings. In this way dispositions and patterns of mental functioning can be set up that are maladaptive and that become pathological. In addition to factors such as conflict and defence analytic developmental concepts such as delay, arrest, disparity, deficit, inhibition, regression, precocity and so on, have all been ways of conceptualizing these breakdowns in development. Pathological depression, which has its own character and power, is one pathway through which these deviations can be given psychological expression.

British object relations theories provide a specialist conceptual version of this theory of development that takes as its focus an emphasis on the interaction between interpersonal reality and psychological reality – both in theory and in the nature and the model of treatment. In the United States object relations theorists utilize the concept of 'object representations' to describe these interactions. Within this theory there are distinctive descriptive accounts of pathological depression in the context of normal depression and a sample of these will be summarized and presented in Chapters 4, 6 and 7.

Impact of personality variables

The predisposing effect of personality organization or personality type upon depression has been long considered but so far the evidence has been inconsistent (Rosenbluth et al. 2005). For example, while conventional wisdom dictates that personality pathology can impact the patient's capacity to seek out, participate in, or be compliant with treatment, Mulder (2002) concludes in his comprehensive review that depressed patients with Axis II personality disorders do not have a worse response to treatment when optimal medication and psychotherapy is in place.

The difficulties, it would seem, lie not with clinical observation but in the methodological challenges of disentangling those factors relating to the personality disorder from those attributable to depression (Roth and Fonagy 2006, p. 192). Nonetheless, models have been developed to explain the interface between personality and depression that may have predictive and explanatory value in describing research. These models deal with factors such as predisposition, pathoplasty, complication and spectrum (Clark 2005).

In the realm of psychoanalysis since the time of Freud, Abraham, Adler and Reich, psychoanalytic theorists have been formative in providing nosological descriptions of character or personality types and their disorders. While the creation of personality types such as neurotic, obsessive, paranoid, histrionic, hypochondriacal, melancholic and dependent can be credited to these pioneers, psychoanalysts have continued to contribute to a basic clinical understanding of adaptive and maladaptive aspects of personality – schizoid and paranoid personality (Fairbairn; Klein); as-if personality and cyclothymic personality (Deutsch); narcissistic personality (Kohut; Rosenfeld); pseudomature personality (Meltzer); borderline personality disorder (Kernberg), and so on. Moreover, in the field of depression the early division into 'neurotic' and 'endogenous' subtypes was based on personality traits. In fact, the comparisons between 'neuroticism' and 'depression' have largely used two personality measures: the Maudsley Personality Inventory (Eysenck 1959) and the Eysenck Personality Inventory (Eysenck and Eysenck 1975).

In modern times the psychoanalyst who has been most prolific in researching the influence of personality traits on treatment resistance in depression has been Sydney Blatt (Blatt 1974; Blatt and Blass 1992; Blatt and Ford 1994; Blatt et al. 1996). As a psychoanalyst he has also achieved the distinction of being the most ecumenical and collaborative of researchers – working alongside cognitive-behavioural clinicians as well as colleagues using pharmacological treatment. Initially, he called theoretical attention to certain interpersonal traits – both cognitive and emotional – with enough rigidity to survive brief treatments and therefore to interfere with remission. This led on to identifying two pronounced personality dimensions as decisive causal variables associated with aetiology, treatment response and prognosis of depression. These dimensions describe patients with strong dependency/need-to-please traits and patients who are overly ideational, self-critical and perfectionists. Using these personality clusters as research tools – dependency/sociopathy and self-critical/perfectionism – Blatt and his numerous colleagues have generated an enormous amount of research that has left no aspect of the study of subclinical and clinical depression untouched.

For example, in his contribution to a major study of outpatient treatment of depression – Treatment of Depression Collaborative Research Program (TDCRP) sponsored by the US National Institute of Mental Health – Blatt et al. (1995, 1996) ascertained that brief treatments for depression, whether pharmacological or psychological, are relatively ineffective in patients assessed prior to treatment as being highly self-critical and perfectionists. On the other hand, patients with low levels of perfectionism were more responsive to all four treatment modalities investigated. Further analyses of the data also cast doubt on the arbitrary nature of chosen treatment periods – in patients with high levels of perfectionism or self-criticism the therapeutic progress stopped in two-thirds of the patients in the second half of the treatment process (weeks 9–16).

While the study of personality or personality traits is vital to assessing treatment response, and therefore prognosis, psychodynamic therapists are principally interested in these variables because their aim is to treat the person not the depression. 'Personality is what one *is* rather than what one *has*' (PDM Task Force 2006). This statement of clinical philosophy would form the central rationale for recommending long-term psychodynamic psychotherapy as the treatment of choice for personality-loaded depression.

The problem of chronicity and relapse

Relapse refers to a regression to prior symptoms following an interval of remission while recurrence denotes a fresh episode of depression – both suggest that depression can take on a chronic pattern. In fact, relapse has been associated with chronicity as well as other factors such as history of episodes; recent trauma or stress; poor social support; interruption of treatment and the sheer complexity of depression. While nowadays relapse is often reported within one to two years beyond treatment, it is interesting, historically, to compare this with the length of period before relapse in earlier populations of depressed persons, with repeat episodes occurring anything between ten and twenty years later (Beck and Alford 2009, p. 54). This confirms that depression was once an episodic illness whereas nowadays it is commonly judged to be a lingering problem with a number of possible courses. This is borne out by the view often expressed nowadays in the mental health community that remission, and not recovery, should be the goal of treatment. Given that as human beings our biological composition has changed very little in the past one hundred years, how would such a development be explained?

The question of inappropriate treatment approaches has remained little explored critically, especially by those with vested interests in certain treatment modalities that have dovetailed so well with popular research designs, as exemplified in the randomized controlled trial (RCT). Within this empirical format the most widely tested treatments for efficacy for depression are the structured brief treatments such as CBT, IPT, BDP and, of course, antidepressant medication.

The results of comparative testing of the efficacy of long-term psychodynamic psychotherapy has been a slow work in progress but more and more informative, well-controlled and relevant studies are coming on stream. For example, Stiles et al. (2008) replicated a previous study comparing CBT, person-centred therapy (PCT) and psychodynamic therapy (PDT) using a much larger sample and found, as the previous study had done, that theoretically different approaches tended to have equivalent outcomes. Then in comparing short and long-term PDT, Knekt et al. (2008) concluded that in the depression group short-term PDT created faster benefit but that this was significantly reversed during a three-year follow-up by better outcomes in the long-term cohort. Similarly, in a meta-analysis of twenty-three psychotherapy outcome studies, Leichsenring and Rabung (2008) added that short-term PDT was insufficient for patients with complex mental disorders, that is, patients with chronic mental disorders or personality disorders and that long-term PDT produced far superior effectiveness.

Yet the best tested, mainstream therapeutic modalities must be questioned. This may not be a popular step, but some account must be given for the fact that as depression reaches epidemic proportions worldwide current treatment pathways using SSRIs (even with maintenance pharmacotherapy) and brief treatment formats, or both, produce no more than 50 per cent success in remission rates. Of course, the reasons for this alarming development may be multifarious – involving possible social, economic and, of course, ideological factors such as reliance on critical mass treatment options – but what responsibility should be ascribed to treatment methods themselves? Taylor (2008) argues that of all the psychological illnesses, depression is the least suitable for assessing the effectiveness of treatment through short-term randomized controlled trials. When considering a broader range of evidence, Taylor concludes that two strong trends are clearly evident: all the short-term therapies, including short-term psychodynamic therapy (PDT), are more or less equivalent in benefit. However, these benefits have a ceiling when compared with long-term psychodynamic treatment which produces more lasting effects by absorbing social, personal and work-based impairments.[3]

Shifting to antidepressant therapy, other researchers believe that the popularization of the biochemical theory of depression has been an unqualified disaster. Kirsch (Kirsch 2009; Kirsch et al. 2002, 2008), for example, is convinced that the theory that depression is caused by a chemical imbalance in the brain is in crisis. He cites the following number of ideological and empirical factors: large placebo effects in the treatment of depression, especially in patients with initial severe depression in their response to medication; the significant distortion of research findings by the proven withholding of negative results in published drug trials funded by drug companies; the risk of 'serotonin syndrome' when more than one SSRI is prescribed or where they are taken with other serotonin enhancing drugs; that the SSRE 'tianeptine' has been found to *decrease* serotonin but does not induce depression which disproves the monoamine imbalance theory; and finally, the high rates of residual depression following SSRI monotherapy.

Having now become a study area of its own, it is probable that relapse prevention will soon be incorporated into treatment recommendations for anyone diagnosed with depression. Why? This trend was initially set by combination SSRI and CBT, first introduced for safety considerations in prescribing antidepressants for children and then, along with IT, to provide some prophylaxis against relapse in adults. The writing was on the wall for the clinical goal of remission, and soon, supported by unconvincing follow-up evidence, a general inference began to creep into the 'Conclusion' sections of research studies to the effect that relapse could be an intrinsic factor in the course of depression. Logically, of course, all that this implies is that relapse is a significant variable in clinical course when *SSRI therapy* is the chosen treatment partner. Pharmacological treatments have a lot to answer for, especially when the best solution that can be offered for relapse prevention is to stay on full dosage medication for an indefinite period, or to enter a maintenance phase for life (Kupfer et al. 1992). The other factor to emerge since the mid-1990s is SSRI withdrawal, sometimes euphemistically defined as 'SSRI discontinuation syndrome', that describes a range of physical and mental reactions that follow the interruption or cessation of treatment or dose reduction. Such reactions usually result in the resumption of medication without any recognition of iatrogenic factors.

It is incumbent upon researchers and academics to rationally explain what is meant by treatment resistant depression. Has the understanding of the structure of depression been oversimplified? Is treatment resistant depression a subtype of depression? Does it follow, say, the same natural course as alcohol or drug addiction? What is clear is that the need for a return to theory appears most urgent on the subject of relapse, and a tentative contribution to the understanding of the phenomenon of relapse will be made in Chapter 9 within an object relations framework.

In conclusion, one model of treatment, already established in the United States but currently being investigated in the UK, that highlights the chronic nature of depression, is 'collaborative care', which consists of a combination of clinician and patient education, consultation liaison between primary and secondary care clinicians and case management, held together by a case manager, who liaises between primary care and mental health specialists (Richards et al. 2009). Unfortunately, the UK National Institute for Health and Clinical Excellence (NICE) guidelines have adopted the same imperious stance to collaborative care as they have done with counselling and psychodynamic psychotherapy – they claim that these are limited options for people who either decline antidepressant or short-term psychological intervention or have not responded to short-term psychological interventions, antidepressant treatment, or a combination of the two. The hidden reason must be the presumed expense of these options but this is not candidly stated.

Chapter 2

Freud's theory of depression

Here are happenings rich in unsolved riddles!
Freud (1933)

The developmental pathway of depression in its descriptive, dynamic, and genetic dimensions was laid down metapsychologically, and to some degree clinically, by Freud and Abraham in the early 1900s. At that time more or less every medical clinical entity touched by psychoanalysis yielded fascinating and ground-breaking psychological results, and depression, even though its existence as an affliction of the mind had been known for centuries, was no exception. Using these early contributions as starter points, this chapter will discuss how the phenomenon and meaning of depression is generally understood psychoanalytically. I shall begin with Freud's initial statement that depression is an inherent feature of the psychoanalytic theory of development. That is to say, depression is a natural occurrence and a living byproduct of the stages of infantile and adolescent development as described by psychoanalytic theory. In other words, depression, as with anxiety, is part of the fabric of mental growth. This will be situated in the context of Freud's classical drive theory in its account of how the mind is activated by the drives through a continuous tension between the demands of these drives and the demands of reality. My goal is to emphasize that during this maturational process depression is a secondary effect of the transformation of narcissism into object love, and to go on to give an account of this transformation within an object relations framework. I shall also be illustrating how the theory draws a distinction between a normal and a pathological or clinical depression. Put briefly, a normal depression has its basis in an average expectable transition from narcissism to object love, but where complications occur this becomes a *neurotic* depression, while a pathological depression reflects a serious obstruction in progressing from the stage of narcissism to object love where the outcome is a *narcissistic* depression. This analysis, in effect, is what Freud set out to do in 'Mourning and melancholia' (1917) where he outlined the basics for an understanding of the psychodynamics of these two forms of depression. This classic has served as the basic psychoanalytic text, and a point of departure, for all subsequent writings and innovations by psychoanalysts on the developmental pathway of depression.

How can depression be conceived as an intrinsic feature of the psychoanalytic theory of development? In explicating this theory it will be necessary to refer to certain foundational concepts in psychoanalysis, concepts that may be familiar, perhaps over-familiar, to the reader. I would like to begin, however, by setting out Freud's drive theory as outlined in *Three Essays on the Theory of Sexuality* (1905) and 'Inhibitions, symptoms and anxiety' (1926) and link it to his thesis on depression in 'Mourning and melancholia' (1917) as a way of explicating the general assumption held by many psychoanalysts that depression, like anxiety, is an elemental feature of psychological development.

The story of the drives and the substitution in primary narcissism

According to Freud, the human organism enters the world with a phylogenetic or biological endowment consisting of endogenous needs that demand satisfaction. These irreducible needs Freud identified as drives and he clustered them into two groups – the sexual drive and the drive towards self-preservation. The self-preservative or ego drive is focused on staying alive and sustaining life. The sexual drive, as Freud defined it, refers to an endogenous force underlying all human activity – which is reflected in the organism's libidinal motivation to satisfy sexual impulses and fantasies. In 1920 Freud modified his dual drive theory into the sexual and aggressive drives. The aggressive or death drive referred to a force of stagnation in the psyche that potentially influences all actions and interactions with the world. While Freud defined the death drive as a force of entropy he also stressed the range of self-destructiveness of the death drive. Both drives in actuality play their part in forcing the mind into existence and forcing it to 'work'.

The individual develops out of the 'exigencies of life', that is, the pressures and demands of the drives in relation to the encroachments and demands of external reality. The drives transmit messages to the body for certain somatic necessities to be met, but the problem is that what is needed does not reside endogenously – it resides 'without'. Therefore, a pairing-up has to take place between these somatic needs that reside 'within' and sources that may be able to fulfil these needs that reside 'without'.

This puts the infant in an implausible situation. It experiences these urgent somatic necessities, yet what it requires to satisfy them exists not 'within' but 'without'. What can the infant do? Freud suggests that the psyche was like an amoeba:

> [T]he pleasure-ego wants to introject into itself everything that is good and to eject from itself everything that is bad. What is bad, what is alien to the ego and what is external are, to begin with, identical.
>
> (Freud 1925, p. 236)

This is exactly the economical solution that the infant employs to remedy the situation – wishful phantasy. The infant simply phantasizes that whatever is needed from 'without' already resides 'within'. In this phantasy, all the biological necessities that require fulfilment in order to survive are arrogated to the 'self', while simultaneously whatever is 'within', aching and agitating to be satisfied is phantasized to exist 'without'. In this way the remedy of phantasy permits the 'object' of internal tension or anxiety or conflict to be substituted by another object that relieves tension, anxiety or conflict – by equation. Freud took care to explain that there is nothing personal about this process. Such is the urgency to solve this afore-mentioned situation that the infant will attempt to settle by any means these urgent somatic necessities – even by using part of its own body for this purpose.

The first substitution

This is the stage of development Freud (1911) described as primary narcissism, dominated by a purified pleasure ego. It could be viewed as an ingenious solution on the part of the infant to the threat of extinction. Translated into a sharper statement of megalomania, it could be added that the pleasure ego determines that all sources of nurturing coexist with the self, while all the demands for nurturing exist in the object. This false unity comes about through a substitution of internal reality for external reality via the use of mechanisms of introjection and projection – introjection of all that is 'good' and projection of all that is the 'bad' (Freud 1915b, p. 135).

Of course, when we examine the infant's canny use of phantasy, it becomes clear that, even though this is in the service of survival, a dangerous precedent has been set. This turns on the fact that the phantasy solution rests on a misconception between inside and outside, and by implication, between self and object. One might be tempted to theorize, as Melanie Klein (1935) later did, that there is a seriously delusional aspect to the psychology of everyday infancy.

The second substitution

The story of the drives continues. Although the solution of primary narcissism is an example of simplicity itself, it inevitably runs into difficulties because it cannot be sustained in the face of the judgement of reality. Repeatedly, the pleasure ego finds itself, against expectation, not cushioned or reinforced from 'without' and these experiences of failure in provision renew the alarm calls. Such calls, however, merely increase the urgency of the somatic drives in a manner that eventually exhausts the infant's reliance on the substitution of internal and external reality.

The infant's new solution, however, is no less innovative. It simply deploys its previous economical solution in a new way. It creates a different substitution, not as before between the external and internal reality, but instead, the infant now splits the previously 'good' object residing 'within' into two making one the 'good' and the other the 'bad'. Applying the same manoeuvre as before, the 'good' one is retained as 'self' and the 'bad' one is located 'without'. By this new substitution the infant can continue believing that all that is 'good' resides in the self – now a part of self – and all that is 'bad' resides outside the self, in the other. This would qualify as secondary narcissism in Freud's terms. For Klein and Fairbairn, as will be discussed later, this qualifies as the paranoid-schizoid dimension to infant development. By both accounts, however, the point has been reached where a psychic agency – the ego – has established itself as the site where drive conflict can now be expressed in psychological terms.

Now Freud's theory of depression, in its normal and abnormal dimensions, is nothing more than what happens next, subjectively, in the course of ego development under the growing impact of the reality principle.

To describe what happens next I shall simply be continuing as I have begun – by outlining further steps in the developmental process of substituting internal reality for external reality as a ballast against 'the exigencies of life'. This will however allow for an eventual clarification of Freud's description of the psychodynamics of two types of depression.

'Psychoanalytic' depression

The claim so far is that depression, like anxiety, arises as a secondary effect of having gradually to forgo narcissism as the price to be paid for adapting to the reality principle. Such a developmental move is resisted, however, through a false unity with the object that is established, first, through a substitution of internal for external reality, followed subsequently by the splitting between the 'good' internal object into two so that the 'good' one can be substituted by the ego for internal reality.

In order for development to proceed satisfactorily, clearly, the infant has to recognize that the object is not 'self', but exists independently. Similarly, the infant has to discover that all goodness is not coterminous with the 'self', and that, in fact, it is possible for goodness to reside 'without'. With this recognition comes the complementary realization that what resides 'within' might also not be all good. Impulses, desires, feelings, phantasies and thoughts emanating from 'within' may not be so beneficent; in fact, they may cause trouble 'without', resulting in states of embarrassment and shame. Hence in reversing the replacement of external for internal reality, and modifying the secondary split of the ego where all goodness resides in 'self' and all badness resides in 'object', a degree of sadness arises naturally in the ego that Freud identified as the *normal self-limiting illness* called mourning. From an analytic viewpoint, mourning is a necessary contingency in the transformation of narcissism into object love.

Object love

However, making the transition from narcissism to object love ushers in a fresh and urgent set of problems for the infant. First, recognizing the loved object as independent holds terrifying risks. It could die, or run away, or fall out of love with you, in other words the object as separate obeys the irreducible laws of the external world. Second, there is the conflict of ambivalence – the clash of the opposing attitudes of love and hate towards the same object – a clash that gives rise notably to guilt. In psychoanalytic theory, therefore, the understanding of depression and its subtypes revolves around the individual's attempts to work out these two problems – the problem of the self and object as independent and the problem of the conflict of ambivalence.

Let us now turn to Freud's famous monograph 'Mourning and melancholia' (1917) where he investigates these questions in depth. This text contains Freud's definitive statement on the loss of a loved one that has been broadened by successive generations of psychoanalysts to include diverse forms of loss. His writing is pure metapsychology and contains no clinical material but the processes and moods described are singularly relevant to certain constant dynamics found in depression. I shall proceed as before by tracing the next step in the substitution process.

'Mourning and melancholia'

Freud describes how coming to terms with the dual problems of the object loss (real or ideational) and the ambivalently loved object can take the subject in two directions. First, the path of mourning which involves a gradual acceptance of the demise of the object through reversing – at great cost emotionally – the attachment process. That is, through undergoing a step-by-step relinquishment of the emotional investment in the object in 'deference for reality'. The excruciating aspect of this experience, says Freud, owes as much to the natural over-attachment to the object immediately following the shock of loss, as to the frequent moving reminders of the object in familiar settings and in dreams. It must be stressed that though Freud emphasized loss as bereavement, he had various losses in mind, real as well as abstract – such as the loss of the love or withdrawal of the love of an object, loss of an ideal like freedom, loss of a country and so on – all these losses disturb the person's narcissistic integrity in a way that is fundamentally depressive.

This path of mourning can be categorized as representing a 'normal' depression in the sense that it is on the road to something. For Freud the optimal outcome of mourning is the ego's freeing itself from the shadow cast upon it by the object's demise – leading to a renewal of the subject's interest in other inner objects as well as the outside world. The other goal is to establish the lost, loved object within the ego as a memory.

To paraphrase, mourning is a disease of the ego where the subject clings to the ghost of the object at all costs as if it were a fetish. 'All the ego's energy is diverted towards the object', leaving the ego spent, as evidenced in the falling off of mental, libidinal and physical function during mourning (Freud 1917, p. 249). This impoverishment of the ego is also reflected in the symptoms typical of depression, the most striking and pervasive being anhedonia.

In other words, the impoverishment of the ego during mourning involves a recapitulation of the regression that occurs as part of the infantile solution of primary narcissism. In phantasy, the lost good object, and all that is needed from this object, is once again arrogated to 'self', and everything that is bedevilling and painful about the loss of the object is ascribed to 'without'. This return to a narcissistic identification is typically reflected in the heightened state of self-preoccupation during mourning, both mentally and bodily. In Freud's conception, the necessary 'work of mourning' involves the gradual accommodation of the reality of loss on the basis of a shift from a *narcissistic* identification with the object to an *introjective* identification of the ego with the object (Freud 1917, p. 249).

Then there is the path of melancholy – meaning 'black bile'. The plight of the melancholic is comparable, says Freud, to the reactions of the mourner 'with one exception' (Freud 1917, p. 244). In parallel with the mourner the melancholic experiences 'a profoundly painful dejection, abrogation of interest in the outside world, loss of the capacity to love, inhibition of all activity, and a lowering of the self-regarding feelings' (Freud 1917, p. 244). But in this type of 'profound' mourning, as Freud described it, the reaction of grief contains a morbid and obsessive quality that has a certain signifi-cance. Yet as in the case of a normal depression, in a profound depression there is a similar return to a narcissistic identification with the object as a means of coping with loss. Accordingly, everything that is 'good' that is needed from the lost object is assigned, in phantasy, to 'self', while every-thing that painful 'within' pertaining to the lost object is designated, in phantasy, as 'without'. Consequently the object has not been lost and the subject can continue relating to it in the same manner as before. Hence the reinstatement of the object in melancholia rests on the reinstatement of primary narcissism.

The 'exception', however, is that in the ordinary mourner, this is a temporary state that will be terminated by the work of mourning, whereas in the melancholic the regression to a narcissistic identification with the lost object becomes a fixation. This means that the lure of reality can do little to shake the subject's ego from clinging to the object and hence the melancholic's suffering can never fully be brought to finality. Freud obliquely mentions another possible basis for this clinging – distinct from the melancholic's regression to narcissism – an unconscious loss of a love object (Freud 1917, p. 245). But overall, it is through exploiting the exceptional factor that Freud arrives at his demarcation of the psychodynamics of mourning from the psychodynamics of melancholia, as well as briefly calling into play a cyclical subtype of depression.

The third substitution

The second factor that Freud noted about the morbid quality of grief in the melancholic was something distinctive about their self-regard. In spite of an intense focus on the self, there comes about a spectacular loss of self-esteem – a type of narcissistic collapse. The person feels himself worthless, dishonest, blameworthy, and morally repugnant and feel the need to broadcast these lamentations to everyone. While such negativism goes hand in hand with the dramatic falling away of instinctual life in depression, in his classical account Freud explained that such self-reproaches and accusations were tied up with the melancholic's strong ambivalent attitude toward his or her love objects that was unconscious. Hence the accusations aimed at the ego were really meant for the dead person, but they were being masochistically displaced onto the ego. They were displaced in order to avoid the terrible guilt that would otherwise surface if the ambivalence towards the object were to be openly felt. So these two factors, the 'exception' of a reinstated narcissistic identification with the object, coupled with a delirious sense of worthlessness due to inverted aggression, were the distinct reactions to loss that Freud believed warranted the diagnosis of melancholia, that is, pathological depression.

To explain why and how melancholics attack themselves so publicly, Freud (1917) outlines yet another ingenious substitution along the lines of previous splits. To recall, there was the original substitution of internal for external reality (primary narcissism), in the second instance there came about a splitting of the 'good' internal object into two – one good and the other bad (secondary narcissism). Now Freud (1917, p. 247) claims that the ego itself develops a split that permits the coming into being of an alternative portion of the ego – designated the 'superego'. The superego, in character, is alienated from the remaining ego in that its tendency is to observe and assign blame to the ego, on all accounts but mainly on moral grounds. Accordingly, in a normal depression, subjectively, the world becomes bleak and empty but in a pathological depression it is the ego that loses its vitality owing to being split in two – the ego and the superego – with one half pitted against the other half. Hence, in summary, the super-ego comes into being as part of the depressive process, developmentally speaking, and its initial function is to invert the mourner's repressed rage towards the lost object by turning it on the self for the express purpose of disavowing guilt.

With this new agency of the superego, it becomes apparent the centrality Freud gave to the role of self-reproach, and defences against guilt, in depression – guilt in relation to the feared loss of love of the object; guilt relating to ongoing ambivalence; and the specific defence against guilt of turning aggression upon the self. Much of this nineteenth-century view of the melancholic's psychodynamics is still very much in keeping with present-day thinking, especially about the role of guilt and aggression in the onset of dysthymia and major depression and its potential for self-destructiveness. Interestingly, some of the unusual symptoms of the melancholic were retained in the DSM-IV as a subcategory of 'Depression with melancholic features'.

Facing guilt: the twin dangers

Yet in edging closer to recognizing inner conflicts of ambivalence two great dangers now await the melancholic. The first is the risk of suicide, should unanticipated anger towards the lost object not be kept below the threshold of awareness – leading to guilt. The act of suicide, or a suicide attempt, would then constitute a last-ditch act of persistence on the part of the melancholic to retain his or her narcissistic identification with the object – even at the cost of self-existence. Such a desperate act would mean that the mad and dangerous solution on the part of the infant (primary narcissism) would have been acted out so successfully that the difference between internal and external reality would have been completely extinguished. This explains why experts often claim that suicide can take place only in a delusional or psychotic state of mind.[1]

The second great danger, should guilt approach consciousness, is the possibility of a switch into mania. In pathological depression the switch to mania arises when the superego begins to tail off its merciless grip on the ego. At that point objective rage towards the lost object may enter consciousness once again raising the spectre of guilt and sorrow, but the slightest awareness of this acts as a trigger for an upswing to mania. The flight to mania therefore artfully defuses a turnaround from self-abasement to object-abasement because of its frightening consequences, and as a result the melancholic is once again let off the hook.

This is illustrated by how the upswing miraculously releases the ego from all its suffering (or pseudo-suffering) from which a great amount of energy is now liberated. Up to this point the ego has become so destitute owing to the loss of instinctual life and to being split into two that when this new energy becomes available it is given over entirely to replenishing the ego, over and over again, and by whatever indiscriminate means. We recognize in this compulsive filling-up or puffing-up process certain states of mind typical of mania – preponderantly oral states: excessive talkativeness, changing the subject, not accepting another viewpoint, racing thoughts, delusions of grandeur, overindulgent forms of gobbling like alcohol or drug abuse, and of course wanton acts of generosity to self or others – the 'feast in mania' as Freud (1921) once referred to it. The mind may be shallow but the mind is on fire, and becomes heedlessly consumed with everything light and frothy so that no thought can be brooked of anything weighty, grave or laborious. What was denied in the melancholic state by the superego is grasped at every turn by the ego in the manic phase.

In this way, in manic states, the ego turns the tables on the superego. Freud (1921) suggests that the ego and superego actually become fused, 'so that the person, in a mood of triumph and self satisfaction, disturbed by no self criticism, can enjoy the abolition of his inhibitions.' This triumph, particularly, is over the conscious guilt aspect of the ambivalently loved object that was lost, and the great elegance of mania as a defence is seen in how cleverly it cuts off the problem of guilt at its root. By devaluing of the importance of the object, by devaluing any love of, and dependence upon, that object, all awareness of the need for the object can be voided. In these enterprising circumstances ambivalence can finally and triumphantly reign! One can take or leave the object with impunity, gobble it up and spew it out, lie and cheat your way around the object – who cares, you can profitably indulge all these attacks upon the object safe in the knowledge that there will be no anxiety, morbid grief or guilt.

The unfortunate coda, however, added by Freud at the end of his brilliant monograph, warns of how in acute mania the breaking off of the relation with external reality can have more grave consequences. A manic-depressive psychosis may be the outcome, reflecting a disintegration of thinking as the speeded-up mind becomes ever more divorced from reality.

In concluding it may now be possible to suggest a definitive summary about the two pathways open to the depressed person dealing with significant loss, real or abstract. In normal mourning there is a regression to *secondary narcissism* to cope with the loss, and because the split is in the ego the mourner is able to solve the problem of ambivalence via *introjective* identification. The melancholic, on the other hand, may cope in analogous ways as the mourner to loss, but cannot resolve the problem of ambivalence because the split is between internal and external reality – owing to a regression to *primary narcissism*. The only identification possible here is identification by *projection*. The 'exceptional' factor together with the severance of the ego from the superego underscores the perilous plight of the melancholic's ego. Through a denial of object loss, and of the conflict of ambivalence, there comes about an exodus to external reality of great conviction; however, a flight to internal reality is also feasible, resulting in states of depersonalization consistent with a loss of contact with external reality.

Freud's metapsychological correlation of mourning and melancholia, taken as a piece of meta-theory, is foundational and has endured as a central formulation in psychoanalytic thought, having radiated out into various conceptual and clinical sectors of psychoanalytic explanation. What is most striking in Freud's analysis is to see how the extraordinary elegance of the original infantile solution to object loss or separateness – the phantasy of primary narcissism – makes its reappearance in the adult suffering from object loss or removal in an insidious and potentially fateful way.

The legacy of Freud's famous monograph is his classification of depression into neurotic and narcissistic depression while suggesting some affinities between the two based on some common features but clear structural distinctions. In terms of a contemporary nomenclature Freud's two subtypes could be considered as overlapping with DSM-IV categories of dysthymia and major depression where the connection between object loss and depression is acceded, though these comparisons may not be productive since psychoanalysis speaks about the 'depressive process' or 'depressive conflict' that like the 'somatic process' or the 'phobic process' are unrelated to duration or persistence or to a list of symptoms, and may cover a variety of clinical realities that are based on specific mechanisms.

A further trend in theorizing was established by both Freud and Abraham by giving oral sadism a first-rank role in the onset of depression in conjunction with the primary significance of the aggressive energy of the superego. *Apropos* this combination, some discrepancy has been pointed out in Freud's formulation about the role of the superego (later termed the ego ideal) in depression by Zetzel (1953), who questioned how it was possible that the superego, which is derived from genital Oedipal conflict, could exist in the pre-genital characteristics of the depressive superego. One possible answer lies in Freud's notion of unconscious guilt that suggests an earlier history for guilt. 'As to a sense of guilt, we must admit that it is in existence before the superego, and therefore before conscience, too' (Freud 1930, p. 136).

Chapter 3

Karl Abraham's theory of depression

The affect of depression is as widely spread among all forms of neurosis as is that of anxiety. Anxiety and depression are related to each other in the same way as fear and grief.

Karl Abraham

Nothing prepares the reader for the sheer scale, lucidity and intellectual rigour of Abraham's writing on depression, except, that is, for Freud's own contributions that have their own individual qualities of being more free ranging and conceptually explorative. Yet what distinguishes Abraham's contribution is its grounding in clinical practice – for this reason his formulations have stood the test of time and to this day they remain compatible with the general body of analytic knowledge about depression (Zetzel 1960).

In his first study of 1911, Abraham reports on six cases that cover a range of mood disorders. He gives the reader a quick entry into the world of the depressive states by describing a young man who at the age of 28 suffered his first attack of hypomania, succeeded by a slump into depression. His account is evocative, especially in describing the patient's symptoms – apathy, loss of libido, self-hatred, pronounced feelings of inadequacy, suicidal thoughts, and nocturnal masturbation that is summed up in the patient's morbid verdict, 'I feel happiest in bed' (Abraham 1911, p. 143). His description is likely to strike a chord with any contemporary clinician working in the field of depression. Abraham gets straight to the point – the patient's symptoms were bedded in repressed hatred, resulting in terrible guilt that was paralysing his capacity to love. Emphatically, Abraham defines depression as a neurosis, rooted in the repression of what he terms 'insatiable' sadism.

Once Freud's monograph 'Mourning and melancholia' (1917) had appeared and been assimilated, Abraham took up the challenge again in 1924, starting off with the similarities between depression and obsessional neurosis. During depression related to loss, Abraham (1924) declared, the subject uses obsessional defences belonging to the anal stage for the purposes of conserving and controlling the lost object. This allows the subject to exercise a kind of compulsive ownership of the object as a means of bypassing certain phases of normal mourning. However, if the sadistic tendencies of the anal stage gain the upper hand – tendencies that attempt to control the object by expelling it and destroying it – this is likely to lead to symptoms of depression. The acts of conserving or expelling, in Abraham's rather imaginative view, make use of the psychic mechanisms of introjection and projection (Abraham 1924, p. 443). He also explains that when depression is on the mend any resurgence of ambivalent conflict causes either a recurrence of depression or a switch to mania. If, however, the obsessive mechanisms make themselves available the switch to mania is averted.

Abraham refers to case material from a patient who after an acute bout of depression entered a period of remission. The baffled patient reported a fresh symptom – of being overcome while out walking by a compulsion to eat faeces lying in the street. Abraham concludes that this was 'a literal confirmation that the unconscious regards the loss of an object as an anal process and its introjection as an oral one' (Abraham 1924, p. 444). He goes on to explain that the patient's phantasy of eating faeces represented his desire to take back into his body the love object that he had expelled by equating it with faeces. What was expelled in hatred anally is incorporated orally but fails to become established as a good object – instead it becomes a persecutory object that yet again has to be expelled, either anally or orally.

In 'Mourning and melancholia' Freud (1917) had asked why the mourner, having carried out successfully the work of mourning, did not slide over to mania? Abraham emphasizes that a switch to mania is more likely during the remission period from depression, that is, when a depression has advanced to the point where the subject begins to feel better. This period takes the form of renewed energy that allows the person to get on with life, to be excited about new projects and to resume interest in family and friends. His answer to Freud is that these are normal states of egocentric exuberance that in excess are clinically equivalent to a manic state. However, should the ego at this time resume an acute conflict with the love object through coercive anal tendencies then the outbreak of energy would follow a reactive manic course.

In the 'frenzy of freedom' that exists in mania, Abraham found evidence of a further regression to the oral stage in depression. This he represented by the two oral tendencies – incorporation to conserve the object and cannibalistic incorporation of the object as a means of destroying it. The expulsion or spitting out the object can, in phantasy, can also be carried out sadistically. Abraham adduced this from the wide variety of oral preoccupations in manic states. 'The patient devours everything that comes his way' (Abraham 1924, p. 472). Furthermore, the regression to an *earlier* sadistic oral conflict with the object can engender a greater intensity in unconscious ambivalence towards the object of loss, resulting in a more painful and debilitating form of depression.

In deciphering the mechanisms and unconscious meanings of depression, Abraham's crucial insights are as follows:

- mania is a customary response to the lifting of depression of all kinds
- when mania is absent following the remission of depression it has been repressed
- both depression and mania have the same aetiology – a hostile expulsion and hostile incorporation of the lost object, except that in mania this cycle becomes compulsive and is driven at a greater pace
- the mechanisms at play in both depression and mania are introjection and projection, used successively and excessively
- the libidinal stages of anal-sadistic and oral-sadistic are implicated in depression and its subtypes
- the switch to mania can be clinically forestalled by providing analysis during the 'free interval' following the lifting of depression.

At the conclusion to his 1924 paper, Abraham produces an impressive table depicting his expanded view of the stages of libidinal development and how they might suggest obstacles and disturbances to normal development. Here he presents himself as a consummate Freudian. The libidinal aspect of oral and anal object relations must be divided in two phases – an earlier pre-ambivalent phase and a later ambivalent phase. In the pre-ambivalent stage the infant is capable of 'partial' love with a 'partial' object while in the ambivalent stage a 'partial' object can be treated with 'partial hate'. The subdivision is quite brilliant in leaving room for a great variety of object relations' permutations, not to mention their relevance in working out how, for good or for bad, later genital primacy bears the stamp of pre-genital impulses and imagos in all their multiplicity.

To conclude, it is impossible to find any psychoanalytic text on depression that does not refer to Abraham's contributions. Zetzel (1960, p. 480) claims that, 'The fundamental blueprints . . . for the psychoanalytic understanding of depressive illness were drawn with amazing accuracy in the classical papers on this subject written by Freud and Abraham.' Abraham's legacy seems to have long outlasted his short but remarkably productive life. His originality was in setting his focus on the mother, and not the father, in understanding the origin of disorders of mood originating in aggression and guilt. This emphasis opened a new chapter of psychoanalytic inquiry into the mother–infant relationship that, in relation to insight into depression, would be taken up with great enthusiasm by other authors such as Radó (1928), Deutsch (1951), Jacobson (1946) and, of course, by Melanie Klein. Doubtlessly, it is no coincidence that they were all his analysands.

The impression one gains is that Abraham was more 'subject' related than 'object' related in his theorizing, that is, he focused on the clinical phenomenology of patient and on the mechanism determining the illness as the main source for his insights and inspiration. It seems doubtful that he wrote about depression from personal experience, that is, if we take seriously Jones' (1927) characterization of him as someone with 'incurable optimism'. At the time of his premature death, however, at the age of 48, he had for nine months been a training analyst to Melanie Klein whose life was deeply versed in the themes of depression.

The question of Klein's 'closeness' to Abraham is obviously a complex one but it is worth considering. He was her analyst at the time of her greatest need, with the return of her own depression following her mother's death. In reading them side by side, one cannot deny the synergy between them, both in terms of his influence on her thinking as well as her impact on his theorizing which he was obviously exposed to through her work with pre-latency children. As regards his influence and support, and her strong sense of gratitude to him that she expressed throughout her life, it may be worth summarizing some of the most interesting and salient examples. These influences are common knowledge; however, they are rarely referred to in the general literature in any detail, except by Segal (1979, p. 204). By going into the detail, the strong identification by Klein with Abraham, indeed her emulation of him, can be brought out, an identification perhaps made more penetrating and lasting as a response to his untimely death.

Abraham was known in the Berlin Society, which he founded, for keeping the focus of meetings on clinical psychoanalysis (Roazen and Swerdloff 1995). He would present his work and give his interpretations and then throw the meeting open for discussion. Others would follow. In reading him too one finds that he rarely yields to theoretical speculation without adding a cautionary note or an undisguised caveat. This emphasis on psychoanalysis as a clinical discipline must have made a strong impression on Klein since the embellishment of her own scientific contributions with case material became a strong feature of her writing, as well as the writings of her students. She may have been less successful, however, in imbibing his circumspection for Byzantine theorizing but then she was never a total believer in staying level with her teachers.

In his 1924 paper Abraham suggests that where an attack of mania occurs on its own, that is, when it is an example of 'pure' mania, the origins must lie in a 'primal parathymia' that has not been overcome in infancy (Abraham 1924, p. 475). In this statement lies a derivation of Klein's concept of infantile depressive illness, as a genetic factor in all later depressive states throughout the lifecycle. Furthermore, Klein's view of mania as intimately related to depression is identical to Abraham's conception and was completely aspirational in her bringing out the pervasive role of mania in all depressions, especially the triumphant aspects of mania. In a similar vein, we can trace a variety of Klein's later formulations to Part II of his 1924 paper, especially the sub-chapter titled 'The origins and growth of object love'. Consider the following statement:

> Complete and unrestricted cannibalism is only possible on the basis of unrestricted narcissism. On such a level all the individual considers is his own desire for pleasure. He pays no attention to the interests of the object . . . On the level of partial cannibalism the individual shows the first signs of some care for the object . . . [though] his desire is still directed towards removing a part of the body of the object and incorporating it.
>
> (Abraham 1924, p. 488)

This way of thinking about part object love saturates all Klein's theories, no more directly than in the conceptual distinction she drew between the paranoid-schizoid and the depressive position. Furthermore, Klein's concepts of 'part' or 'whole' objects must have also had their derivation in Abraham's reference to 'partial love' or 'partial hate' in small children – in relation to 'partial objects' like the penis, breast, faeces. He also asserts that in depression the object can be introjected 'in toto' (Abraham 1924, pp. 497, 490).

The question of influence is self-evident in these illustrations but I think they are best summarized by Ogden's (2003) term of 'bi-directional' influence, in his sense that one needs Abraham to understand Klein no less than one needs Klein to understand Abraham.

Chapter 4

Melanie Klein's theory of depression

Intricate phobias grow
From each malignant wish
To spoil collective life
Theodore Roethke[1]

Melanie Klein suffered from periodic depression. Her depression began with several bereavements during her youth and adolescence – and became a continuous strand running through her life (Segal 1979). These experiences doubtless lent themselves to an intimate understanding of depression, and therefore they played a vital role in the direction of her theoretical explorations as well as in her creative output generally. They would certainly have inspired her best known concept of a psychological substrate for depression throughout the lifecycle.

In 'Mourning and melancholia' Freud (1917) left three questions tantalizingly unanswered – one rhetorical and two substantive. He declared that it was not clear to him why in normal grief the step-by-step detachment of libido from a lost one was so extraordinarily painful, yet sufferers showed such forbearance in absorbing this degree of suffering. He also wondered, parenthetically in relation to the melancholic, whether the degree of suffering was related not only to a conscious loss but also to an unconscious loss of some kind (Freud 1917, p. 245) Finally, he puzzled over why the normal mourner, having surmounted his loss by carrying out the work of mourning, does so without succumbing to an upswing into mania.

Klein (1940) wrote 'Mourning and its relation to manic-depressive states' more or less as a pendant to 'Mourning and melancholia'. She took these questions and fashioned her contribution as responses to them. She contended that there is *both* a conscious and an unconscious loss in all mourning, more so in abnormal mourning, and that the extraordinary pain that Freud referred to was tied to the danger of not only losing the object in reality but also losing the internal representation of the object. She went on to explain that this leads to a situation of inner dread comparable to the infant's fear of death, and that it is this primitive anxiety associated with losing a store of original object representations that helps us to understand why the work of severance in mourning is so poignant – and so often marked by feelings of hopelessness. In other words, the fear is of losing the thing that is loved the most and losing it *forever*.

Klein's (1940, p. 362) far-reaching view was that mourning a loss in adulthood is navigated by methods similar to those used by the ego during infancy and childhood, meaning that in reinstating the lost object following loss and grief the adult was not doing so 'for the first time'. It needs to be emphasized that she included in these calamities real as well as ideational losses – as well as the anticipation of loss. Her writings establish, more than anyone else's, the phenomenon of depressive illness as a natural occurrence and a byproduct of the stages of infantile and adolescent development.[2] She formulated a universal concept of the 'infantile depressive illness' to describe the infant's journey from narcissism to object love together with the anxieties, conflicts and defences that accompany this journey. Hence, in her view one of the differences between normal and pathological depression in adults fell to historical precedent – to how in the past the child has been able, or not, to establish a good internal object on the basis of positive developmental outcomes (Klein 1940, p. 369). She accentuated experiences such as weaning, childhood separations and the loss of a loved one to substantiate her ideas and like Abraham, Radó and Nacht, she was formative in assigning the origins of depression to the early relationship with the mother. This charted the way for her to conclude that a recovery of the specific lost object in adulthood via introjective identification involves more than the recovery of one object but a circle of internal objects that had been attained in childhood.

All psychoanalytic writers, starting with Freud, have emphasized the essential place of narcissism in depression (Rosenfeld 1959). Freud (1917) noted that the melancholic's plight of 'profound' mourning is characterized by a regression to primary narcissism through which loss was denied in the form of a narcissistic identification of the ego with the object. This identification with a dead object is most clearly evidenced in the ego depletion and appalling loss of self-esteem in the melancholic. In examining Klein's theory of depression, it is important to clarify her ideas on narcissism and her understanding of its role in depression. Narcissism reaches back to infancy and since Klein views depressive illness as intrinsic to specific stages of infantile development the detail of her object relations theories are important. Furthermore, such an exploration will illustrate how Klein established two theories of depression – depression in the paranoid-schizoid position and depression in the depressive position.

Klein's theory of narcissism: the paranoid-schizoid position

Klein saw no reason to distinguish between primary and secondary narcissism. For her the object 'without' becomes the repository not only for somatic pain but also for painful *states of mind*. In her theoretical schemata therefore narcissism comprises a primitive object relation that is urged upon the psyche by death anxiety associated with separateness. This conception of the narcissistic object relation as a defence is pivotal throughout her theorizing and its role in depression can be considered from three vantage points – external to internal dynamics, internal dynamics and dialectic dynamics.

External to internal dynamics

Klein grouped all feeling states in relation to experiences with objects – initially part objects – into two categories. She stressed that these were based on libidinal and aggressive experiences with external objects that led to the formation of two independent narcissistic objects in the psyche – the good object and the bad object. One acts as a repository for positive experience while the other for negative experience. In addition, the situation is regulated according to two principles – pleasure/unpleasure principle and the principle of whether objects are internalized in love or hate. All unpleasurable experiences tend to be associated with bad objects, while pleasurable experiences are allied with good objects. Similarly, all good experiences internalized in hate take up residency in the bad object, while all objects internalized in love find a home for the good object. The creation of these two objects is based on the identical narcissistic process described in Chapter 1 – 'Everything that I need/love is me (good object) and everything that I don't need/hate is not me (bad object)'. This process delineates how in Klein's scheme narcissism characterizes the way the infant constructs its own object, as a defence against object relations that are too frightening or cannot be relied upon. These are essentially the external dynamics of the paranoid-schizoid position

Internal dynamics

Whenever a negative experience arises in the internal good object this is split off and projected by means of an omnipotent phantasy into the bad object (other). This is not only for the purposes of homeostasis but also for survival and for growth. Positive experiences may also, in omnipotence, be projected into the bad object as life giving. Henceforth, the bad object operates independently in the psyche of any type of environmental failure that might result from exposure to a negative experience associated with an external object. Apart from what it acquires from the good object, the bad object feeds mainly on bad objects. This is how it satisfies its own conditions for growth and mental ascendancy, which includes projecting bad objects into the good object. The good and bad objects are therefore in a continual tussle for dominion over the mental apparatus – for growth and for control of the organ of consciousness. This tussle ultimately determines the fate of a person's internal object relations. These are essentially the internal dynamics of the paranoid-schizoid position.

Thus the genesis of the good and bad object is the result of the infant's adjustment to life outside the womb according to two forms of narcissism – positive narcissism under the ascendancy of libido and a destructive form of narcissism under the aegis of aggression.

Dialectic dynamics

When under the predominance of aggression, narcissism takes on a destructive aspect that reflects a distortion of the projective–introjective process by which positive narcissism was founded. The determining factor according to Klein (1932, p. 150), following the path set by Abraham (see Chapter 3), is the incorporation and expulsion of the object in a state of uncontrollable hatred. This lends a pernicious aspect to the projective–introjective cycle that has to do with bad objects reproducing themselves in an atmosphere of persecutory anxiety, especially in circumstances where the good external object cannot be borrowed for reassurance. It is possible that this inner situation, that depicts a surfeit of bad objects, is associated with the typical panic attacks that often precede the onset of depression.

Hence, a preponderance of bad objects in the psyche satisfies the conditions for destructive narcissism expressed as a turning against the libidinal connection to objects. In the worst case scenario the recycling of bad objects creates a paranoiac universe from which the infant can only escape through endowing the external world with less and less interest. This entirely deforms the attachment mechanism that in small babies can trigger early signs of depression in the form of apathy (Klein 1936, p. 305).

Paranoid-schizoid depression

The dynamics of positive and negative narcissism in the pre-ambivalent phase of the paranoid-schizoid position can now be applied to an understanding of the anatomy of pathological depression. What happens when the 'good' object is introjected in hate instead of love? This question was investigated in great depth by Abraham (1911, 1924) in an attempt to describe how a 'good' depression converts into a 'bad' depression. He attributed to the melancholic a cyclical part-object relations set-up where the object, in phantasy, is expelled anally, devalued by being equated with faeces, and reintrojected into the ego as a bad object (Abraham 1924, p.

444). This mechanism, he pointed out, has an earlier incarnation in the second oral phase where the object is incorporated cannibalistically, to which the continuous suffering of the melancholic can also be ascribed.

Klein set her focus on the earlier phase of oral sadism and asserted that should the object, in phantasy, be introjected in hatred then the balance of forces immediately shifts towards a danger situation internally in relation to the experience of introjection. This results in a major anxiety situation. She went on to describe a similar recycling dynamic as her mentor Abraham in which the 'good' object from 'without' is 'torn' or 'gnawed' upon entry which causes the introjection to miscarry in the sense that the introjected object is then experienced as persecutory to a degree that it too becomes something 'bad' that must be expelled 'without'. In other words, where the oral object has been introjected and attacked simultaneously the intense anxiety that arises sets in motion a malignant cycle of projection and reintrojection of 'bad' experiences, whenever they have their origin in excessive hatred. It would be correct to classify this cycling as resulting in *failed* introjections since their effect is to provide little in the way of buttressing the good internal object – in fact the opposite occurs, a gradual denuding of the good object occurs to the point where it is in a continuous state of dilapidation.

This situation produces the kind of despair seen in the melancholic who is never free of persecutory guilt owing to an identification with the dilapidated internal object.[3] While this comprises a significant source of dilapidation there is, as Freud (1971) had identified, another source of dilapidation. He explained how a portion of the melancholic ego separates out into the 'superego' as an attempt to deflect any negative feelings away from the lost object. Self-torment and self-persecution therefore replaces the terrible guilt that would have arisen from ordinary resentment and anger towards the lost object. For Klein, the early superego represents the original independent part-object that forms itself in the psyche in response to bad experiences – the eponymous 'bad' object. Its explicit function is to serve the aims of destructive narcissism – in which the self is not loved, as in the case of the good object, but hated and victimized. This antagonistic portion of the ego, marked by a singular quality of cruelty, comprises the original source of persecutory anxiety and dread in all object relating, and it demarcates paranoid-schizoid depression as a persecutory depression. Freud described this sadistic aspect of the superego as embodying 'a pure culture of the death instinct'.

In these circumstances Klein (1935, p. 27) was keen to point out that the appearance of manic defences is not uncommon – as a flight from paranoid states. This is illustrated in the way the paranoid person becomes 'anorectic' in the sense of being suspicious of external objects. However, in mania the introjective process is so skilfully indiscriminate that all forms of anxiety associated with introjection (and projection) can be quashed – persecutory anxiety as well as depressive anxiety. Klein looks upon the manic defence as the only mechanism that straddles both paranoid-schizoid and depressive position depression; though in the latter it takes a reparative form.

These are the essential dialectic dynamics of the paranoid-schizoid position where the primary good and bad objects, representing two forms of narcissism, fail to co-mingle because of their competition for space in the psyche – reflecting a state of diffusion between the life and death drives. In summary, it can be stated that depression arising in the pre-ambivalent paranoid-schizoid position derives from five sources: first, when good objects are projected into an environment dominated by bad objects, second, when the good object identifies with projected bad objects, third, when objects are introjected or eliminated in hate, fourth, when good objects are destabilized by a noxious introjective–projective cycle, and finally, when the noxious cycle causes a de-cathexis of the mother through the absence of projective identification. These sources are directly linked in one way or another to the characteristic mechanisms operating in the paranoid-schizoid position – splitting, idealization, projection, and identification by projection.

Klein refers to the suffering of the good object in the paranoid-schizoid position in terms of persecution and paranoid anxiety – persecution follows the identification with bad objects while paranoid anxiety reflects the dread of harbouring damaged or dead objects. The depression that results from these two forms of suffering is distinguished by persecutory anxiety and persecutory guilt.

So, in Klein's judgement, the melancholic undergoes a paranoid-schizoid depression characterized by destructive narcissism. This type of depression, a persecutory depression, is based on an unconscious attack on the lost object that is simultaneously preserved through an identification by projection – a type of negative narcissistic manoeuvre that short-circuits the emotional work of mourning through a denial of loss. The fact that the melancholic's suffering is interminable proceeds from a similar type of identification with an internal object in perpetual suffering. The object's suffering, typified by persecutory guilt, stems from, first, its harsh treatment during the processes of projection or introjection, second, by unconscious attacks that persist obsessively long after the loss of the object in the disguised form of masochistic behaviour, and third, from a dangerous introjective–projective cycle that undermines the ego's consolidation of its supply of good objects and diminishes its contact with reality.

To conclude, I would like to suggest that the classic symptoms of depression associated with the pre-ambivalent phase of the paranoid-schizoid position could be categorized as follows. Where the object has been introjected and attacked simultaneously, the dilapidation of the ego frequently takes the form of bodily suffering. Hence paranoid-schizoid depression is predominantly a *vegetative* depression since its origins lie in the immature psyche that cannot yet fully absorb bodily excitation and tension. On the model of the melancholic, the body in pain provides a replacement for the lost object. Symptoms related to physical retardation are therefore prominent – hypochondriacal fears, loss of energy, heavy legs, back pain, constipation, intolerance of noise and bright lights, weight loss, circadian disruption, insomnia or hypersomnia, somatic tension in the body leading to exhaustion, and so on (see Chapter 4). These symptoms usually follow an attack of anxiety rising to panic – the classic onset of a clinical depression – which is associated with persecutory or paranoid states arising from an identification with bad objects, or a dread of accommodating lifeless or dead objects. On the other hand, where the ego is dilapidated as a consequence of merciless treatment at the hands of the superego the symptom profile leans more towards *psychomotor* impairments – foggy brain, agitation, poor concentration, memory loss, stiff body movements and slow speech.

Depressive position depression

Characteristically the depressive position takes as its object the loved and cherished object. But this is an object in possession of subjectivity, with inner moods and feelings that awaken in the infant a terrible discovery – that the mother's care is dependent on her love. This determines that the predominant anxiety shifts not only to a feared loss of object, but also to the loss of the object's love, which means we are now explicitly in the domain of mourning. This change in relation to the object augurs an emotional crisis externally and internally.

External to internal dynamics

It is the 'real' object as an independent object that now defines the dynamics of object relating. A rejection or threatened rejection, a loss or threatened loss of the object, or of its love, takes centre stage and the depressive effect is entirely different. The anxiety focus alters too – retaining the bond with the object becomes paramount and this includes the need for reassurance by keeping the object in sight and by searching the object for signs of well-being. These are the external dynamics of the depressive position and they illustrate the adjustments in the narcissistic object in the direction of object love.

Internal dynamics

Ambivalence is not the same as sadism, which characterizes the object relations of a paranoid-schizoid depression. Yet guilt is an elemental factor in the depression peculiar to the depressive position, and the conflict between love and hate, and its resolution, plays a critical role in what is termed 'depressive guilt'. The distinctive attributes of depressive guilt are feelings of disquiet, concern and empathy for any offence done to the object in the course of object relations – and to react anxiously in an attempt to ameliorate this harm. The drive is to overhaul such a situation and to make amends by putting things to right. But the principal emotions are similar to those experienced by the mature mourner – a stifling of emotion, worry, sadness, pining, guilt, in deference to the reality of object removal. Hence the subject in this type of depression has a clearer view of the variation between phantasy and reality – a form of depressive realism.

Dialectical dynamics

In a 'whole' object environment, there is less need to be preoccupied with bad objects. They may yet continue to be subject to projection but there is a change of purpose with an emphasis on their modification or for their safekeeping by another object. For example, a patient suffering from acute depression brought to his session his entire bedside drawer of medication and left this with his therapist in case his despair tempted him to ingest the lot.

This reaction to despair suggests an internal situation characterized by decreased schizoid functioning and where the projection of bad objects is less tainted by aggression, leading to a dwindling of inner and outer perse-cution. The internal situation is not without strife however, but this now takes the form of a conflict over contradictory impulses. A new cycle of a more benign nature can now be discerned which centres on the struggle between love and hate. These feelings find themselves in such close proximity that where the battle swings in the direction of hate there is realistic concern about harm and a switch to remedying the situation. The repair work can sometimes take on a superficial dimension when mania intervenes to deny negative consequences, yet, otherwise the desire to restore breathes new life into the object relationship and occasions a swing back in the direction of love. These are the dialectical dynamics of the depressive position and they describe the adjustments necessary in resolving the conflict of ambivalence brought on by the advent of 'whole' object relating.

I would like to suggest that the symptomatic picture associated with depressive position depression is by and large characterized by *mental* pain associated with the conflict of ambivalence and guilt – morbid anxiety, excessive rumination and self-doubt, hopelessness, sadness, pining, anhe-donia, withdrawal, attacks of conscience (guilt), masochism, suicidal flashes. Of course, in any depression we find a disruption to both mind and body as reflected in an amalgam of both mental and bodily symptoms. This means that in a typical major depression there are likely to be oscillations between characteristics of paranoid-schizoid and depressive position depression. These oscillations form the basis for a cycling phenomenon when mania intervenes as a defence against mental or bodily pain, and in this way depression becomes chronic. This is essentially the hidden structure of depression that is uncovered with remarkable reliability in the analytic treatment of a depressed person.

In summary, depression arising in the depressive position derives from three sources: first, from states of anxiety, sorrow and pining for the object where the external and internal environment is dominated by ambivalence, second, from depressive guilt arising from a conflict over contradictory impulses, and third, from the undoing of a stable introjective identification with the object by manic defences. These sources are directly linked to the characteristic mechanisms operating in the depressive position – introjective identification, denial, and upswing into mania.

The manic position

The most common form of escape from depression in the depressive position is the marshalling of manic defences as a means of triumphing over the entire scenario (Klein 1935). Freud had asked why the mourner, having successfully carried out the work of mourning, did not slide over to mania? Following Abraham, Klein's rejoinder was that manic states are the rule rather than the exception, and that even in normal mourning there are states of elation interspersed between sadness and distress. She declared that there were recurrent switches to manic states during and after every depression and these are integral to the *structure* of depressive illness.

Klein clearly theorizes a more interdependent relationship metapsychologically between paranoiac, melancholic and manic states. This is the most distinguishing feature of her theory that essentially constitutes a modified theory of cyclothymic states. The question in Klein's mind was less about how the melancholic changes over to mania but how the mania reverts to melancholia. In answering this question she again followed Abraham's supposition that mania represses depression, therefore a true recovery from depression rests on a successful dismantling the manic defences. The manic defences were regarded by Klein as so pervasive that she elevated them to a 'position', that is, not a stage or phase of the depressive process, but intrinsic to the overall resolution of infantile conflicts whether paranoid-schizoid or depressive in nature.

In conclusion, as part of organizing her theories into a more coherent framework, the concept of a universal infantile depressive position, with its characteristic anxieties, conflicts and defences, became Klein's (1940) centrepiece. Accordingly, her theory became a genetic theory that asserted that depression occurs throughout the lifecycle and has its roots in mental struggles stretching back to infancy that can replicate themselves in the mature person in adapted forms. Furthermore, depression and anxiety are indivisible and are a natural occurrence and a secondary effect of the stages of infantile and adolescent development that accompanies the journey from narcissism to object love. At opposing ends of the journey lie paranoid-schizoid depression and depressive position depression. The central factor in pathological depression is the failure to establish the first love objects – the parents –as stable internal objects in the psyche which naturally give the child a sense of inner security though its confidence in the parent's love. It also gives the child a sense of inner companionship that eases experiences of loneliness.

It should be noted that this proposition that developmental life events can give rise to depression essentially began with Freud and Abraham, and it constitutes a particular strand of psychoanalytic theorizing about depression that was taken up and extended by a variety of psychoanalytic writers, such as Radó (1928), Jacobson (1946), Spitz (1946), Deutsch (1951), Winnicott (1954) and Bowlby (1960). Other psychoanalysts approach depression quite differently. Bibring (1953), for example, asserted that depression is unresponsive to the vicissitudes of aggression, while Nagera (1970) stressed the important differences between depression in separation and depression in actual loss.

Chapter 5

When the body gets depressed: Henri Rey

This short chapter presents an object relations formulation of the unconscious meaning of somatic symptomology in depression.

Depression often presents as a psychosomatic crisis. The physical suffering and immobilization of the body – its systems and its organs – are well documented as a way in which depression manifests itself, and indeed presents itself for treatment, particularly in hypochondria. Freud (1917, p. 253) himself pointed out an important somatic factor in noticing how the melancholic's mood lifts towards evening time – one of the first references to the analytic literature to the circadian shape of depression. How are these invasive symptoms, that invariably take a vegetative and psycho-motor form, to be understood analytically? In Chapter 4 it was claimed that the classic bodily symptoms of depression are associated with the deepest level of the mind, namely, the object relations conflicts belonging to the paranoid-schizoid position. That is to say, the body is the principal site of suffering because the ego is not yet sufficiently advanced to fully absorb bodily excitation and tension. I also suggested that where conflicts between the ego and superego are a significant factor in depression symptoms express themselves mainly through mental impairments.

Freud (1892) described depression as an 'internal haemorrhage'. In terms of the body, this seepage can be itemized according to time-honoured symptoms associated with depression – in severe depression: tiredness and sluggishness, pervasive loss of zest and pleasure, loss of appetite, early morning waking, metal taste in the mouth, spontaneous crying, loss of motivation, forgetfulness, eyes sensitive to light, pacing up and down, band of anxiety across the chest or stomach. In less severe depression: overeating and weight gain, oversleeping, heavy legs, tingling arms, backache, cloudy brain, feeling hopeless, and oversensitivity. What is the state of internal object relations that determines these manifestations of depression? I have selected the contribution of Henri Rey (1986, 1994a, 1994b), who adds something special to an object relations' explanation of bodily symptoms in depression. His comments will be supplemented with a theoretical analysis by Meltzer (1960, 1963).

Mental pain and organ pain

Rey (1994a) believes that depression reflects profound changes in the psychic organization of the self and he takes exception to the view that depression should be treated in a biomedical model without taking into account the psychological superstructure of the person. To regard patients as worse when they are depressed, and better when they are not, is a naive error, he suggests, because the reasons for the change are indispensable to the management of the patient medically and to the patient's personal understanding of depression (Ray 1994a, p. 203).

Rey takes a special interest in identifying the unconscious meaning of the vegetative symptoms in depression and exploring what they mean. His contention is that the less and less alive the depressed person becomes, and the more withdrawn, the closer the patient's mental situation resembles a particular type of object relation organization. Rey points out that in relation to object loss, this organization is a defensive organization of which a number of coherent and definitive statements have previously been proffered by the psychoanalytic community.

Freud (1917) and Abraham (1911, 1924), for example, while taking a different emphasis yet establishing a core blueprint, defined depression (melancholia) as a response, on the one hand, to object removal characterized by a regression to a narcissistic identification and, on the other hand, to a deep unconscious ambivalence towards the object. This essentially summarizes the defensive organization in depression and the task of making conscious both the mourning and the ambivalence becomes a significant analytic goal. For Freud, the loss factor (including the loss of the love of the object) followed by a defensive narcissistic identification with the object was the main emphasis, in addition to untiring attacks upon the lost object disguised as self-criticism. For Abraham the incorporative/expulsive process was critical, especially when coloured by oral and anal sadism. Clinically, when the inner object constellation is damaged, the mood of the person becomes depressed.

When discussing the somatic dimension in depression, Rey too concentrates on the mechanisms of incorporation and expulsion of the lost object in a mood of ambivalence, which he reminds us leaves the internal object in a state of ill health or death. He stresses that the dual theory of destructive incorporation through oral sadism and expulsion through anal sadism is especially relevant to the vegetative process. That is because the vegetative states, especially those involving the gastro-intestinal system, are corollaries of an identification of the depressive's ego with the dilapidated or dead products of these oral and anal sadistic attacks.

In this way Rey (1994a, p. 195) attempts to elucidate how the mental conflict in depression is represented by *organ* pain. However, he is keen to represent two sides of the conflict – the identificatory as well as the reparative side. He considers that while the somatic symptoms in depression are the consequence of damage done in phantasy to the object, with whom the depressed person identifies, it is also the case that the functional slowdown in the depressed person physically represents an attempt on the part of the ego to *moderate* this destructiveness by sparing the object further suffering. Thus while the retardation in bodily functions reflects an identification with an object in ill health, it equally represents an attempt by the depressed person to curb any further oral, urethral, phallic, anal and genital aggression towards the lost object. In other words, the slowing of body movements, the lessening of oral activity, oversleeping, the prevention of outpourings of destructive faeces though constipation and the waning of sexual impulses to avoid sadism during intimacy; these textbook vegetative symptoms of depression, as proposed by Rey (1994a), also represent psychobiological attempts at sparing the object further ill health in addition to trying to effect a repair.

The implication is that in some forms of depression the role of ambivalence towards the lost object is a deeper and a more complex dynamic issue involving both destructive *and* reparative phantasies. This accords with Klein's later view that depression belongs aetiologically to the depressive position and its conflicts. In sparing the object further violence, in phantasy, depressed individuals spare themselves from going beyond depression into despair.

In another article, Rey (1994b) illustrates this dual process by referring to some fascinating clinical material from a case discussed by Klein (1935) in 'A contribution to the psychogenesis of manic-depressive states'. The case concerned a severely depressed man with marked hypochondriacal anxieties. I would like to introduce more details from this case study to draw out how she understood the links between aggression, depression, organ pain, and reparation.

Klein describes one dream in which the patient was travelling in a railway carriage with his (much older) parents, who needed his care (Klein 1935, p. 279). In the dream he urinates into a bowl but feels awkward about doing so in front of his father because of his large penis, which he feels might humiliate his father. But simultaneously he feels he is sparing his father the trouble of getting out of bed himself and urinating! In the second dream a kidney sizzles in a frying pan and the patient is so concerned that the sizzling sounds like a live creature being burned alive that he urgently tries to draw his mother's attention to it. Frying, in the dream, was apparently worse than boiling or cooking in the oven. The patient associated the frying to torture methods used in the time of King Charles, such as hot oil and beheadings. Another association was to the oven door that was shut – could it conceal a fire? When reporting this dream the patient complained he had been feeling ill, his head was heavy, his ears were blocked, and thick mucus was pouring out of him. Klein draws attention to the castration attacks on the father in tandem with the concern for the father's feelings. There was also an attack on the mother's body (penis/babies inside the shut oven) that stirred in the patient a worry about setting his mother on fire. She concludes:

> The phantasy of keeping the kidney and the penis alive while they were being tortured expressed both the destructive tendencies against the father and the babies, and, to a certain degree the wish to preserve them.
> (Klein 1935, p. 282)

This is essentially Rey's analytical understanding of the unconscious meaning of the somatic dimension in depression, and the type of object relation organization that underlies it. He therefore gives consideration to the full dynamic role of ambivalent conflict in depressive states, especially as they manifest themselves in organ conflict. This clarifies that in depression somatic manifestations of ill health, especially those taking a vegetative or psychomotor form, have a psychological aetiology and that any chemical imbalances associated with this retardation process cannot be its cause but must be a consequence of the depressive process itself. Nowhere does the depressive process reveal itself more profoundly as a mind/body schism than in its somatic manifestations.

Meltzer on organ pain

In depression, how do internalized object relations gain access to the organs of the body? To explain this Meltzer (1960) returns to the introjective and identificatory processes that Freud, Abraham and Klein placed at the centre metapsychologically of their concept of depression, as well as other forms of psychopathology. He reiterates that objects are internalized by the mutual processes of introjection and projection coupled to the phantasies that accompany them. The fate of these introjections is determined by whether they are motivated by phantasies of cooperation or phantasies of aggression which naturally influences their effects (Meltzer 1960, p. 58). Similarly, internalized objects also become ensconced through projections by external objects and here too they may have different effects depending on whether they have been driven by destructive or benign phantasies. In general, in those cases of hostile introjection by the subject or aggressive projection by the object it is aggression dominates the introjective process. The reverse is true when the mode of introjection is characterized by love and cooperation.

But how does an introjection under the sway of greed or sadism or jealousy have any influence over a body organ or system? Meltzer (1960) maintains that a thorough conceptualization of the internalization process is necessary in order to understand how internalized objects have access to the body and to body tissue. He describes a two-stage process – one involving a dynamic from outer to inner reality and another dynamic between internal objects (Meltzer 1960, p. 57). First, when an introjection occurs under the aegis of oral sadism this leads to bad objects being installed in the psyche. These objects are not ephemeral – they do not float around without purpose but gravitate towards specific parts of the mental apparatus that can put them at their disposal. This, he suggests, is the intermediate step by which bad objects become lodged in the psyche before they can gain any currency for the body. The currency is established when the ego identifies with the bad (or good) object.

Access to the body is therefore achieved via mechanisms peculiar to the ego. In the case of repression, the bad object reappears as an anxiety symptom or a conversion symptom. In the case of more primitive mechanisms, the bad object is subject to the processes of splitting, projection, and identification by projection that reappears as hypochondria. In the case of depression the bad object is a manifestation of the pain of loss and the conflict of ambivalence that is projected into those organs and systems providing essential life support. When the ego identifies with such an object a shadow is cast upon the ego that causes certain body functions to deteriorate – as represented in vegetative symptoms and some psychomotor disturbance such as generalized restlessness.

In this account it is critical to realize these are the same systems that are loved, cared for and maintained during development by the ordinary devoted parents, hence they are associated in the psyche with internal and external parental objects. Any ill health that is incurred by these objects with which the ego identifies can be expressed in superficial or chronic bodily aches and pain or in organ pain.

These, briefly, are the object relations dynamics that govern the somatic process in depression. In many instances the qualities of the bad object determine their effects – they can 'suffocate', 'bite', 'strangle' or they can take control of an organ (Meltzer 1960, p. 59). As far as organ selection goes, this may turn out to be specific to the individual; however, there may be uniformity according to the nature of depression. Freud's notion of 'somatic compliance' would apply, in which case the unconscious meaning of the organ could be worked out in analytic work – the emphasis in depression being on an aggressive cathexis that is displaced onto an organ.

Chapter 6

Winnicott on depression

The tree
Mother below is weeping weeping weeping
Thus I knew her
Once, stretched out on her lap
   as now on a dead tree
I learned to make her smile
   to stem her tears
   to undo her guilt
   to cure her inward death
To enliven her was my living
The sins of the whole world weigh less than this
   woman's heaviness.
             D. W. Winnicott (Rodman 2003)

If Winnicott were alive and practising today as a paediatrician (or a child psychiatrist) he would most probably find himself in hot water. Having recourse in his treatment of depression almost exclusively to a talking cure, direct observation and case management, he would be deemed highly eccentric by his colleagues armed as they are nowadays with the DSM-IV and a battery of state-of-the-art antidepressants. For him the brain, particularly the child brain, was less the organ that required 'tweaking' in the service of cure than the natural developmental pathway, that with the right setting in place could be coaxed back on track. He made his views absolutely plain in his attacks on shock therapy, or 'treatment by fits' as he scathingly called it, when asserting that emotional disorders like depression were essentially independent of brain tissue disease. No one could claim to know, he insisted, how ECT worked in depression, and this implied a turning by doctors to magic instead of science – a view that fits perfectly with the present-day controversial use of antidepressant medication for children and adolescents. The magic in this instance lies in assuming that the successful experiments on the adult brain automatically confer benefit for the developing brain. In general, Winnicott made a habit of championing the 'positive' qualities of depression, both in children and adults, about which he wrote from a mass of clinical experience with considerable authority and enthusiasm. Yet he often used the term 'depression' inconsistently, referring to both health and pathology thereby giving the impression of straddling a political divide (see entry on 'Depression' in Abram 2007).

It was Melanie Klein's theory of depression that initially made a deep impression on Winnicott. In this regard he and Fairbairn were opposites; while Fairbairn found common ground in the metapsychological nature of the paranoid-schizoid position, Winnicott had a more natural feel for the depressive position. What struck him particularly in Klein's (1935) paper 'A contribution to the psychogenesis of manic-depressive states', written in the wake of her son Hans's sudden death, was the paramount attention she gave to the standpoint of the 'inner world' of the child, especially in relation to the experience of weaning. This 'inner world' emphasis subsequently became for him a central feature of his theorizing as 'a thing in itself' (Winnicott 1988, p. 85).

The 'inner world' meant the developmental world and for Winnicott this specifically meant emotional growth and the development of subjectivity. Mental illnesses, he contended, were not diseases like scurvy or smallpox, but were related to the circumstances of a person's emotional development. Accordingly, psychological health and illness had to be located within the continuum between emotional maturity and immaturity or prematurity, and the fluctuations therein. Hence Winnicott located depression somewhere between psychosis and neurosis and in his nomenclature he distinguished between reactive depression and schizoid depression (Winnicott 1963, p. 222). A reactive depression is one that occurs in reaction to life and its problems, in which depression can be a healing factor. In a schizoid depression the engagement with life has been curtailed leading to states of depersonalization, unreality of feelings and a sense of hopelessness that resembles certain features of schizophrenia. While Winnicott once claimed that Klein had changed psychiatric classification by differentiating two kinds of depression, he saw more clinical danger in paranoid-schizoid than in depressive position depression (Winnicott 1963, p. 129).

His first major statement on depression appeared in 'The manic defence' (1935) written as a qualifying paper for the British Society. In this statement he was faithful to a fault to Klein's views on the impact of mania on psychic reality. Historically, when writing about mania psychoanalysts have invoked many arresting images: Freud (1917, p. 255) compared mania to the man who 'runs after new object cathexes like a starving man after bread', while Abraham (1911, p. 151) came up with the image of mania as resembling a 'frenzy of freedom'. Winnicott's paper is evocative and bursts with novel descriptions of mania, especially elevating images ranging from the penis rising, to the balloon as a contra-depressive symbol of mother's over-burdened breasts, to the Ascension of Christ and his text has rightly become a favourite in everyone's psychoanalytic library. His descriptions of the feelings and sensations of depression in terms of 'colour' are also refreshing, as is his account of 'omnipotent control' in mania as 'suspended animation'. His most original statement on mania, however, would appear several years later, when he wrote about the child's manic defence as a reaction formation to the mother's disturbed inner reality (Winnicott 1948).

His description of mania as 'the notorious holiday from depression' appears in his 1954 paper 'The depressive position in normal development', which, as the title suggests, takes as its emphasis the healing aspect of depressed mood in the depressive position – as a counterbalance to depressive illness as such. The paper represents both an advocacy of the concept of the depressive position – he was pleased with Klein's favourable comments (see Winnicott 1969) – but simultaneously it signals a departure theoretically in a number of ways from her formulations. For example, depressive anxiety and guilt, as he describes them, are not merely understood as a response to the internal conflict of ambivalence but to a conflict with the actual mother as she encounters 'the full tide' of the baby's instinctual experience – and her methods of dealing with it. But he continued to believe in the destructive power of mania upon inner reality, 'Few of us', he wrote, 'are innocent of depression, and if we have escaped it we may have done so by a contra-depressive defence which is more abnormal than the frank depressive phase of a patient' (Winnicott 1989, p. 538).

Theories of depression

In Winnicott's writings therefore one finds evidence of two theories of depression – one rooted in Klein's concept of an 'infantile depressive position' and another, developed with more energy after 1954, based on the mother's personality, her moods and her methods of childcare. Both theories were 'inner world' theories but the second gave more weight to qualities of the environment.

In his first theory Winnicott (1954, p. 275) was quick to quash the suggestion that the depressive position meant children get clinically depressed. He stated categorically that the latter was an affective disorder while the former was a phase of development that for clarification purposes he termed the 'stage of concern'. However, regarding the reaction to loss, he discussed the relationship between the two. In the stage of concern, he asserted that, if the child had established a secure position based on introjecting good experiences he would cope expectedly well with loss and would need minimal environmental support in sorting through the ordinary emotions of grief and sadness. However, if the negotiation of depressive position tasks foundered then the balance of forces internally shifts in a persecutory direction and this results in a pathological depression.

In this sense Winnicott is consistent with Klein in theorizing that there are factors that predispose the child to depression – factors that are intrinsic to the tasks of the depressive position. In particular, the tasks of resolving conflicts of ambivalence, which if they miscarry precipitate a regression to danger situations associated with the paranoid-schizoid position. In this however he seems to locate depressive illness in the child in the paranoid-schizoid position that he associates not with guilt but with states of dissociation, and a sense of futility linked to the development of a false self (Winnicott 1954, p. 272).[1] In parallel he claims that in the depressive position, depression is 'a healing mechanism', in that the depressed mood, linked to holding guilt feelings, blankets the entire inner situation and buys time for the personality to organize its own spontaneous recovery.

This comment reflects a long-standing reliance in Winnicott's theorizing on the natural curative processes in development in order to counterbalance an emphasis on pathology, for which he at times invented his own terminology. This distinctive meaning-making was obviously influenced by his paediatric experience and we find it dotted throughout his writings through prefixes like 'in health' or 'in illness'. Holding in mind developmental defences as well as neurotic defences allowed him to conceptualize cases in subtle and often surprising ways. Consider the statement that 'Depression is the illness of valuable people' by which he meant such people's value was in allowing themselves to be burdened with their responsibilities – like a mother who is burdened with concern for her baby (Winnicott 1989, p. 538). This must be a 'good' depression since the person is valuable because he or she can hold a mood and in doing so 'suffer' his or her own illness. In children too, their value was in finding and using transitional objects to overcome developmental depression.

But this ushers in Winnicott's second theory of depression linked aetiologically to the example of the depressed mother who cannot 'suffer' her own depression.

'Please doctor, mother complains of a pain in my stomach'

This statement, says Winnicott, exemplifies a serious problem of childcare when the mother confuses her hypochondriacal depression with her real concern for her child. He claims that in many cases the child's depression is a simulacrum of the mother's depression and that this occurs when the child has been drawn into becoming a constituent in the mother's organized defence against her own depression (Winnicott 1948, p. 91). An identification with the mother is elicited, creating guilt-by-proxy, which leads the child to assume a certain responsibility for the mother's illness. This is followed by an attempt at cure through false liveliness and false reparative gestures. Conversely, the child may take flight into the mother's depression to escape from his or her own depression – a reaction formation (Winnicott 1948, p. 92). The complete theory invoked by Winnicott (1960) to explain this clinical phenomenon is based on the concept of the 'true self' – a new theory – which he developed as a general theory of the primitive emotional development of the infant but with specific applications.

In this theory Winnicott declares that the baby, if he or she is to develop optimally, needs the mother (and the father) to perform three critical functions during the stage of maximal dependence: to bring the world to the baby homoeopathically so the baby can be active in its discovery; to be resilient and non-retaliating in the face of omnipotent instinctual experience; to reflect the infant's gestures and states for what they are, and not for what the mother expects them to be. All three functions combine to allow babies to experience themselves as subjectively 'distinct' and 'true' – in order to make a start 'on his own life' (Winnicott 1948, p. 93). On the other hand, if the mother is preoccupied (depressed) or unresponsive or over-responsive, or if she retaliates when confronted by the baby's instinctual experience, or if she borrows from the baby its nascent vitality this robs the baby of the opportunity to be 'true' and coerces the baby to comply with the mother's expectations. This leads to a social facade version of self for the purposes of survival. In an organized form a 'false self' represses the 'true self' that expresses itself in a variety of clinical conditions.

In the case of the depressed mother,[2] depending on the nature of her depression, Winnicott describes the circumstances in which her adaptation to the baby is foreclosed by a personal need for contra-depressive liveliness. '[T]he mother's need for help in respect of the deadness and blackness in her inner world finds a response in the child's liveliness and colour' (Winnicott 1948, p. 93). Yet the infant or child's over-solicitousness through simulated buoyancy conceals the fact that, through identification, the child can internalize the mother's (or father's) depression as its own. As a consequence, the child loses something elemental to its narcissistic integrity that can manifest itself in depressed mood coupled to feelings of grave self-doubt, hopelessness and alienation.

Ogden (2001) asserts that with his theory of interpersonal depression, Winnicott struck out in an entirely new direction from both Freud's and Klein's accounts of depression. This is true from the point of view of aetiology, and it reflects a distinctive spectrum in analytic theorizing that ascribes to the mind of the mother (object) a specific indispensable role in the growth of the baby's (self) mind. In other words, the infant discovers aspects of its own mind in the 'other'. Such an intersubjective concept of mind is to be found with different emphases in contributions such as Lacan's (1949) 'mirror stage'; Bion's (1962) 'container/contained' model of the mind; Laplanche's (1976) claim that the ego is formed from the primary perception of a fellow creature; Fonagy's (1991) concept of 'mentalization'. On the subject of depression, Pedder (1982) has ascribed the phenomenon of 'interpersonal hopelessness' to a two-person relationship, in which one part feels good about another, that has not been adequately internalized.

Depression in children

Winnicott wrote about child depression with a degree of freshness and jurisdiction that inspired many other clinicians in their belief that most states of childhood unhappiness are self-limiting and therefore call out for a patient-centred approach. Especially in describing symptomatology, he chose to focus on clinical actuality and not on textbook classification as a means of spotlighting the differences between adults and children with respect to clinical presentation.

While in agreement with the basic truth that depression is about mood, he emphasizes that in children this fundamentally takes the form of *defences* against depression, such as 'common anxious restlessness' and 'forced levity' (Winnicott 1975, p. 87). Depressed children tend to cry in a fragile way, are accident prone and display hypochondriacal anxieties about their bodies because they do not dichotomize the physical from the mental. Moreover, they get sick but they also rub their eyes with such intensity as to cause an infection. Hence, they act out their unhappiness or they organize a denial of depression rather than being able to describe it to the doctor. To drive home the point, they typically stop working at school and try running away from home. These are clearly not the symptoms normally associated with adult depression. Again, Winnicott (1975, p. 87) emphasizes the value of symptoms for self-correction – hypochondriacal concerns are signs of life and crying is physiologically valuable if it releases sadness. Similarly, 'emptiness is a prerequisite for eagerness to gather in' (Winnicott 1989, p. 94).

Importantly, however, of all the defences against depression and depressive anxiety Winnicott (1935) paid special attention to the defence of mania. It may be worth looking at one of his cases in this paper to illustrate the clinician at work with the personal meaning of depression and with the equally personal endeavours in taking flight though mania. This is the case of Billy, a 3½-year-old only boy of estranged parents. Billy's mother was depressed and fighting a drug addiction. Billy's main symptom of restless acquisitiveness in life had brought him no satisfaction and led him to stealing money. He over-excited himself in his sessions by shooting pirates and by being shot by his therapist, following which he would fly off, carrying himself over the countries of Africa. Becoming omnipotent in one session, at the end of the hour, he let himself down in the lift but was terrified when the lift took him to the basement. Luckily his therapist, aware of his exalted state, followed him secretly and was on hand to reassure him. Only when the fighting off of enemies in the sessions was replaced by sadness could constructive play take place. The therapist is clearly alive to the environmental factor of the mother's self-preoccupation in anticipating the patient's need to be found.

Nowadays, the research into the effects of maternal depression upon infants is a thriving growth industry. One important impetus came from the Winnicott Research Unit at the University of Reading where Cooper and Murray (1998) reviewed the research on the effects of postnatal depression on the mother–infant relationship. These effects on the child's cognitive and emotional development were found to persist till the age of 5, and the significant factor linking postnatal depression and adverse child developmental outcome was the impaired pattern of communication between mother and infant.

In conclusion, it can be said that Winnicott employed a surplus of meaning in his conception of depression. Overall, two theories of depression can be identified in his writings, as opposed to observations of depressive 'effect' or 'mood' or 'tendencies' which are sub-theories relating to developmental maturities in terms of ego strength. His first theory linked clinical depression to the paranoid-schizoid position while his exposition of the depressive position placed an emphasis on depressive mood as a normal feature of the stage of concern, though he occasionally acceded to Klein's formulation that depressive affect occurs in both. He found greater clarity, however, in his second theory where he could supplant Klein's criteria with his own, based on the concept of the failure of maternal provision, which he had already begun in his 1954 paper. His central criterion here was the attainment of 'unit status' to decide healthy or pathological depression. Briefly, he theorized that the infant becomes a unit before the time of genital dominance when he 'becomes able to feel the self (and therefore others) to be whole, a one thing with a limiting membrane, and with an inside and an outside' (Winnicott 1988, p. 67). This, he stated, is already an advance on the environmental–individual set-up where little or no differentiation exists between inner and outer reality. Ideally, it is the mother who assumes the environmental aspect of the total set-up and who facilitates the move to 'unit status', and the pivotal moment for this facilitation process occurs during the experience of weaning.

In essence, Winnicott is describing the transition from primary narcissism to object love similar to Freudian theory but shorn of some of its vocabulary and its drive theory. Depression, as the capacity for sadness and self-doubt, and depression as a withdrawal to 'non-unit status' (disintegration) due to the failure to tolerate wholeness, are both potential outcomes of the maturational process. Winnicott too, therefore, represents in his views the object relations assumption that depression, like anxiety, is an inherent aspect of mental growth: a natural byproduct of the stages of infantile and adolescent development.

Chapter 7

A note on Fairbairn's concept of 'futility'

> The reverse side has a reverse side.
> Japanese proverb

> The mind is its own place, and in itself
> Can make a Heaven of Hell, a Hell of Heaven.
> Milton, *Paradise Lost*

A sense of hopelessness, helplessness, impotence and exasperation are all well-documented affect states in the clinical presentation of depression. They may even represent a subtype of depression. When writing about these states, psychoanalysts from different theoretical traditions tend to group them in various combinations but their intention is to emphasize the overall *burden* that depression places upon the psyche. However, there appears to be no rubric under which these similar states can be gathered for the sake of theoretical neatness. I think Fairbairn provides the ideal home for all of them, for the reason that with his evocative concept of 'futility' he comes closest to depicting the ontological mental agony that is implied in this particular pathway to depression.

As Rubens (1998) points out, Fairbairn never developed a distinctive theory of depression – in fact, he became conspicuously uninterested in the subject. He suggests that Fairbairn's writings on depression must be viewed in terms of his general approach to psychic functioning, that is, as a 'very general mechanism of conservation of the endopsychic situation and stasis in the closed system of experiencing the world' (Rubens 1998, p. 222).

To define what Fairbairn means by 'futility' it is necessary to give a brief summary of his theory of psychic structuralization. However, this is necessary for quite a separate reason, namely, to illustrate how, according to Fairbairn's account, a sense of 'futility' is an inexorable outcome of the way of the way the psyche itself is structured.

Fairbairn's innovative aim was to describe the establishment of the child's basic endopsychic situation freed from Freud's theory of the drives.

In its place he proposed a theory of personality development centred on the relationships between the ego to its objects, both internal and external (Fairbairn 1949, p. 153). Like Freud, he began with the intolerable situation experienced by the infant when parental provision is less than optimal and therefore frustrating. To Fairbairn this is the first paradox the infant faces – of the mother who both satisfies and deprives, who brings hope as well as hopelessness.

As Fairbairn conceived it, the infant's initial solution, in the service of survival, is to remove the frustrating mother (object) from the external world by placing it 'within' by the mechanism of internalization. In this way, the infant achieves a double aim of mastering the frustrating object and preserving the external object for future satisfaction and love – at the self-sacrificial cost of acquiring the frustrating object for itself. This is conceived by Fairbairn (1952, p. 66) as the 'moral defence'. However, for the infant this method of jurisdiction over an intolerable situation soon presents a new paradox. With the frustrating or unsatisfying object now ensconced 'within', the internal environment now comes under threat and in mitigation of this threat a new solution must be sought. This involves the splitting of the frustrating internal object into two endopsychic structures – the rejecting or anti-libidinal object and the exciting or libidinal object both of which are repressed. Again, the motive is to safeguard the perception of the good object as a love object in perpetuity, but on this occasion at the cost of splitting the self – a variation of the 'moral defence' that is characterized by destructive narcissism – the bad object that is taken in is idealized which gives it impunity in its opposition to the libidinal object.

A point of exasperation is now reached. Having reproduced the problem proposed by reality as a problem of endopsychic reality the hapless infant nonetheless continues to be assailed by experiences of frustration and disappointment at the hands of his mother. This further paradox forces the infant into a final act of helpless self-sacrifice – fearing that he cannot be loved, or be connected to the object, he deduces that it is his love that causes these rejections and accordingly he blames himself in a mood of futility.

Hence a sense of 'futility' derives from the fact that the very means by which the infant sought to preserve the good object unwittingly creates a deeper isolation from that object of love and understanding. In Fairbairn's estimation, the experience of futility is therefore a structural component in the formation a schizoid mode of being – a structure consisting of the two endopsychic structures of the anti-libidinal object and libidinal object whose dynamics henceforth hold dominion over personality development. As far as they can be successful as defences against futility, Fairbairn (1952, p. 213) nominates two forms of omnipotence – mania and schizophrenia – both of which, however, lead the subject further and further away from the destination of object love.

But Fairbairn (1958) does not let the matter rest there. In addition to the libidinal ego and the anti-libidinal ego he theorized a third ego – a central or reality ego that could judge whether the external object was truly frustrating, or whether such frustrations were merely temporary and therefore rectifiable through reassurance by the object. This implies that, in ideal circumstances, it is possible for the central reality ego to open up a pathway to the environment for the pursuit of object love. Such a prospect, however, is an anathema to the libidinal and anti-libidinal egos that owe their existence entirely to keeping a closed system for the purposes of survival. In fact, such are the constraints placed on the free operation on the central reality ego that its natural objects in the external world have no choice other than to become idealized objects. It transpires that Fairbairn, in his theory of endopsychic structures, will not allow any deterrents against futility; they are all follies except for those occasions when the schizoid mode of being can be transformed into object love. This journey of hope, however, is made all the more arduous, some would add impossible, by the virtually total segregation of the inner world from the influence of reassuring environmental objects, even idealized ones. In which case the journey to object love itself may be a facade for a journey into the 'heart of darkness'.

Clearly, there are many opportunities for depression to flourish in this deeply fatalistic account of psychological development that pushes to the limits the fundamental psychoanalytic assumption that ego development, in structuring its necessary defences, produces pathological states. To a greater or lesser degree this is a theoretical feature of all British object relations theorists who attribute a potentially self-defeating dynamic to early developmental scenarios – pre-eminently, in the way in which the psychoanalytic 'object' itself is constituted. The claim is made that in its mode of inception there is something intrinsic to the psychoanalytic 'object' that ensures its 'unavailability'.

As outlined above, Fairbairn's 'moral defence' traps the subject in a lie about the nature of the object from which emerges a sense of loneliness, hopelessness and futility. Comparatively, such a lie is also evident in how Winnicott's 'False self' is constituted, in the form of a colonization and imprisonment of the 'True self' from which a sense of futility must surely flow. Consider too the parlous state of affairs for the infant in Klein's paranoid-schizoid position, where bad objects are reproduced in the psyche though a recycling of hostile projections with hostile introjections that trap the infant in an emotional situation of despair. Klein, however, addressed this phenomenon at a different level of explanation derived from her belief that the infant or child was capable of the type of unconditional hatred that could lead to a persecutory type of depression, whereas Fairbairn, like Winnicott, described a situation of conditional hatred.[1] Nonetheless, all three theorists are at one in asserting that the mechanisms by which the infant seeks to secure its survival during the early structuralization of the psyche, when put to excessive use, can tragically place at risk that very survival and growth, through defining 'survival' not as a need for a unitary or central self, but as a need to maintain initially two closed subsystems of the self, that should develop only in parallel. This inescapably leads to depressive affect.

However, the theorist whom I believe most resembles Fairbairn in his tragic view of the development of personalized object relations is Lacan. He too addresses himself to the inadvertent alienating effects that transpire from the manner in which the psychoanalytic 'object' is constituted. His theory of the 'mirror stage' exemplifies this ontological dilemma of a primordial 'lack' in the genesis of object relations (Lacan 1949). In looking in the mirror, he asserts, the infant is captivated by an image of wholeness and integration that surpasses its own undeveloped state but which the infant identifies with, and takes as a prototype of its ego. In this way the ego is formed on the basis of a lie in the sense that it is not a representation of the self but of an ideal self – an 'other'. All future identifications undertaken by the ego resemble this pattern and they merely serve to ramify an alienated conception of the self. Consequently, in life, the individual takes on the features of an impostor, ceaselessly searching for reconciliation with the true self through the medium of 'others' – even to the extent that the subject's desire is predicated on the desire of the other. Yet when the search remains and continues to be saddled by the specular prototype of the 'mirror stage', this only adds further grades of illusion to the imaginary ego. The ontological situation of longing for the subjective self, therefore, cannot be resolved and the individual, pushed by the 'lack', is left with no other choice than to be pulled into the artful and capricious world of language in the search for an inner reality. This detour can provide only exponential opportunities for self-defeating experience.

In their different ways Lacan and Fairbairn capture a sense of the destiny of the psychoanalytic object as elusive and unattainable by virtue of the fact that the very means by which the subject seeks to establish the object, unknowingly creates a deeper segregation from that object. They both begin with the state of helplessness (*Hilflosigkeit*) in the infant, and end with a sense of helplessness and futility that characterizes an ontological impasse. They too begin with helplessness as the keystone of anxiety and end with helplessness as a harbinger of depression. In summary, both the theory of the 'schizoid mode of being' and the theory of the 'mirror phase' are theories of how the ego is structured in destructive narcissism under certain conditions that encapsulate how the passage to object love is rendered a difficult if not a virtually implausible goal.

Nothing at the centre

Fairbairn (1952) concluded, controversially, that in clinical practice those patients who are normally diagnosed as 'depressed' should more accurately be described as suffering from a 'sense of futility'. Futility is caused by the failure to secure the love of the object and to safeguard this love notwithstanding every effort so to do, including self-sacrifice. He described the result as

> a complete impasse, which reduces the ego to a state of utter impotence. The ego becomes quite incapable of expressing itself; and, in so far as this is so, its very existence becomes compromised . . . the characteristic affect of the schizoid state is undoubtedly a sense of futility.
>
> (Fairbairn 1952, p. 51)

A sense of hopelessness, helplessness and impotence in relation to unrealizable wishes and longings in securing basic needs has long been advocated by several psychoanalytic writers as distinctive states of mind representing certain pathways to depression not necessarily related to loss. In essence, such writers define depression as a pathology of the wish. Fairbairn's concept of 'futility' fits in with this strand of theorizing, nonetheless for him basic needs are defined in terms of the wish for essential closeness rather than a wish for the object *qua* object. In Chapter 8 I shall be suggesting that Fairbairn's emphasis on the object *relationship* adds a radical element of resigned fatalism to this strand of thinking about depression.

To conclude, the concept of 'futility' may seem a narrow one but when taken as an umbrella term, it amounts to something more substantial than the sum of its parts. Nevertheless, Rubens (1998) regrets that Fairbairn's rejection of 'depressive position' depression from his basic explanatory paradigm led him to ignore depression altogether. The implication is that by preferring to a total psychology of the schizoid position he overlooked the fact that Klein had attributed distinctive manifestations of depression to schizoid situations as well.

Chapter 8

Analytic subtypes of depression

In this chapter I would like address the question of psychoanalytic sub-categories of depression, and to correlate and compare the conclusions reached, or implied, by object relations theorists such as Klein, Winnicott and Fairbairn with those of Freud's original conception. This comparison will then be broadened to a sample of writers representing other theoretical orientations within psychoanalysis concerning their considerations on subtypes. Some comments will also be made about how these subtypes overlap, or not, with DSM-IV categories.

Freud's legacy to the future psychoanalytic understanding of depression has been a complicated one. In his classic statement in 1917, he gave us two subtypes depression based on distinct psychodynamics – a neurotic depression on the model of mourning and a narcissistic depression modelled on the melancholic. In Chapter 1, I summarized the dynamics of Freud's two pathways thus: in neurotic depression there is a regression to secondary narcissism, and owing to the fact that because the split is in the ego the mourner is able to solve the problem of ambivalence, revenge and guilt via introjective identification. This solution ordinarily ameliorates the acute nature of the depression in the direction of recovery, as is discovered in analysis. In a narcissistic depression the regression to a primary narcissism reflects a substitution of external for internal reality, hence object loss or removal is voided and with it the central problem of ambivalence and guilt towards the lost one. Indisputably, the watchword of the melancholic is denial but this does not mean the melancholic ceases from suffering – on the contrary, the suffering suffuses all mental and physical areas of the melancholic's life much like a clinical depression. A large area of this suffering, as Freud explains, is self-inflicted and takes the form of public rants against the self. But these attacks, he adds, are yet another manoeuvre to neutralize the conflict of ambivalence through inverting hostility towards the self. That is, the melancholic treats his ego as if it were the object that had so cruelly abandoned him. These dynamics of self-infliction, according to Freud, explain the suicidal ideation and tendencies found in this subtype of depression.

Freud ends his monograph by referring to the only remaining two avenues open to the melancholic if he should persist in his narcissistic identification as a means of denying loss and the anger that accompanies loss. The first takes the form of an exodus to external reality – a manic escape by the ego from the indomitable shadow of the object. The second comprises the denial of last resort that can bring about the most parlous consequences for the ego – a total flight to internal reality that removes all contact with external reality.

These are the central ingredients of Freud's legacy to our understanding of depression related to loss, real or abstract, founded in psychic conflict, regression to oral aggressive incorporation of the object, aggression turned against the self, and an accent on the interrelationship of depression and mania.

In Chapter 2, I outlined how Klein, similarly, proposed two pathways to depression that further emphasize the problem of anxiety and guilt – 'paranoid-schizoid' depression and 'depressive position' depression. Depression in the paranoid-schizoid is distinguished by persecutory and paranoid anxiety – persecution follows the identification with bad objects while paranoid anxiety reflects a dread of sheltering damaged or dead objects. The feature of most note is the mode of identification – which constitutes an identification by projection. This determines that paranoid-schizoid depression is a manifestation of destructive narcissism.

In the second pathway depression arises from states of sorrow and guilt over a conflict between contradictory impulses that are indicative of an external and internal environment dominated by ambivalence. Here the distinctive affect is depressive guilt, linked to an introjective identification with the object, marked by feelings of anxious waiting, concern and empathy towards the object. In the case of developmental loss (as in weaning, or as in renouncing the love object of the Oedipus complex, or as in a midlife crisis loss) the depression resembles in many ways a bereavement process. However, Klein gave considerable weight to how the effects of depressive pain can activate manic defences, which may result in a regression to paranoid-schizoid functioning.

In Chapter 2, I also suggested that the classic symptoms of depression in the paranoid-schizoid position are predominantly *vegetative* in nature since their origins lie in the deeper layers of the mind. On the other hand, the symptomatic picture associated with depressive position depression is revealed in *mental* impairments owing to the conflict of ambivalence and guilt – morbid anxiety, withdrawal, apathy, excessive rumination, sadness, longing, anhedonia, attacks of conscience, inverted hostility leading to thoughts of dying and a wish to nullify a wrong. I also added that in any depression we find a disruption to both mind and body as reflected in the amalgam of both mental and bodily symptoms. Hence in a typical major depression we are likely to see oscillations between characteristics of paranoid-schizoid and depressive position depression, and this is exactly the clinical picture that most often emerges in the analytic situation. These oscillations, furthermore, form the basis for a cycling phenomenon when mania intervenes, as a defence against mental or bodily pain.

The other factor to highlight is the close relationship in Klein's theory between anxiety and depression which is very much the contemporary view – that just over half of people suffering from anxiety disorder go on to develop major depression. Whether her emphasis is on persecutory, para- noid or depressive anxiety, such anxieties are adjudged as the precursors of depression.

In roughly comparing Freud and Klein's formulations there are grounds to suggest that Freud's neurotic depression is Klein's depressive position depression, while her paranoid-schizoid depression resembles his narcissistic depression. These distinctions reflect a common prevalence given the role of narcissism in depression and its influence on the type of depression preceding, and following, its transformation into object love. There is, in addition, a common assumption that mania is a complicating factor in converting neurotic depression to narcissistic depression.

In the case of Winnicott's understanding of depression he pressed for the concept of a continuum for depression stretching from everyday depression in the service of health to clinical depression characterized by personality factors that included a vulnerability to mania and parasuicidal states of mind. Hence, he situated depression somewhere between psychosis and neurosis (Winnicott 1963, p. 222). In his first theory he advocated two subtypes of depression – reactive depression that occurs in response to life and its problems, in which depression can be a healing factor, and schizoid depression in which the engagement with life has been curtailed leading to states of depersonalization, unreality of feelings and a sense of hopelessness that resembles certain features of schizophrenia. On rare occasions he agreed that depressive position depression could have clinical features, however, he continued to include mania as an inviting alternative to depression in all his statements on depression. His second theory was an interpersonal theory founded on the exemplar of the infant's tie to a mother with a concealed depression. Winnicott comes close to the concept of a narcissistic depression when describing mood disturbances before unit status, compared to the structure and phenomenology of depression once unit status is attained.

Fairbairn's concept of 'futility' has more of an affinity with Freud's later comments on depression and I would like to discuss the significance of his concept against the background of a different emphasis given to the con- ception of depression by a wider range of analytic contributions.

I have in mind the contributions developed within the ego psychology tradition. Some of these writers, informed by Freud's structural theory, questioned whether his aetiological emphasis on regression to oral aggressive incorporation of the object, guilt and aggression turned against the self, applied to all forms of depression. Prominence should also be given, they claimed, to other common factors unrelated to aggression and guilt. They took as their focus comments made by Freud in his 1926 contribution 'Inhibitions, symptoms and anxiety' where he reformulated his theory of anxiety and added an addendum to his previous reflections on the affective state of the depressed person. Returning to the melancholic's dilemma, he adduced that the most salient emotional response to the psychic pain and anxiety associated with loss (and separation) is a 'longing accompanied by despair'. This he qualified as an 'unsatisfiable cathexis of longing', that is, a wish for the indispensable object that cannot be realized. From this arises a sense of mental helplessness that the loss can never be undone, leading to a depressive state (Freud 1926, p. 171).

Thus was born a 'helplessness theory' of depression. Following this theme Fenichel (1945), Bibring (1953) and Jacobson (1953), asserted that the core structure of every depression was a loss of self-esteem. Bibring, accordingly, insisted that depression was solely a disease of the ego, and he shunned the idea that psychic conflict or aggression could play any vital role in depression. He maintained that when assailed by states of helplessness and powerlessness, dating back to the struggle during infancy for narcissistic supplies, we should expect a depressive reaction in the ego, as we would expect an anxiety response to trauma. Loss of self-esteem in depression is particularly destructive, he emphasized, when the ego is helplessness in realizing aspirations and ideals, such as, the ideal to be loved. That the ego gets depressed is borne out by the general retardation in psychomotor functioning during the onset of depression.

Sandler and Joffe (1965), in their search for a common aetiological factor in depression, specified that the self-esteem in question refers to an infantile ideal state of safety and well-being that, if unattainable, causes a depressive reaction.[1] This reaction is marked by a sense of helplessness in relation to the object tie. In putting forward this proposition – that a discontinuity between the infant's actual and ideal state of the self produces depressive affect – they in fact sought a unified conceptualization of Freud's classical and structural theory of depression. In both the classical account of depression related to loss, characterized by regression to oral aggressive incorporation of the object, psychical conflict of ambivalence and aggression turned against the self, as well as in depression defined as an ego state that expresses a loss of self-esteem due to helplessness in achieving wished-for aspirations, they postulated a common factor: the painful loss of an ideal state in the relationship with the object. They added that the earlier the depression occurs the more likely this will be constituted as a narcissistic depression because the greater will be the person's search for an infantile ideal state of satisfaction. Implicit in these developmental considerations lies a distinction between two subtypes of depression – an anaclytic (narcissistic) depression and an introjective (neurotic) depression founded on defences of differing maturity.[2]

To return to Fairbairn (1952). He preferred the term 'futility' over 'depression' to describe what he maintained was the central trauma in evolution of a schizoid mode of being: the failure to secure the love of the object, and to safeguard that love, notwithstanding every effort so to do, including self-sacrifice. The result was an ego shrunk to a state of helplessness and hopelessness. The benefit of Fairbairn's conceptualization is that it provides a thoroughgoing object relations account of the origins and dynamics of helplessness, an account that implicates helplessness in the dynamics of ego formation itself. That is to say, in Fairbairn's theoretical scheme helplessness is endogenously generated during the structuralization of the psychical apparatus. Freud's originally used the term helplessness (*Hilflosigkeit*) to describe the fact of absolute dependency of the infant on the (m)other, and the implications of this for the development of fantasy and psychic growth generally. However, he later gave it a structural aspect when he instated helplessness at the core of his second theory of anxiety related to the ego's response to internal as well as external danger. In his concept of 'futility', I believe, Fairbairn exemplifies this structural aspect especially as it applies to Freud's 'unsatisfiable cathexis of longing', thereby giving a deeper resonance to the clinical manifestations of these states of mind in depression. Hence, in my view, it should be an umbrella term under which other aetiological references to helplessness/hopelessness as they relate to the loss of self-esteem in depression should be grouped. It should be noted that this approach is implicit in the developmental assumptions of all British object relations theorists – that depression, like anxiety, is a natural psychobiological occurrence that originates in the natural stages of infantile and adolescent development.

Mention must be made of research perspectives on the subtypes of depression. Since the 1970s, up to the present day, Blatt and colleagues (Blatt 1974; Blatt et al. 1976; Blatt et al. 1990; Blatt et al. 1995) have found ample theoretical and clinical evidence for the conceptualization of two subtypes of depression – an Anaclitic (dependent) and an Introjective (self-critical). Anaclitic or dependent depression is expressed in the libidinal realm of interpersonal relatedness and originates in feelings of loss, isolation and helplessness in dealing with fears of abandonment. Introjective or self-critical depression reflects ideational problems in establishing, protecting, and maintaining a viable sense of self in the face of a punitive superego that stimulates anxieties about guilt, failure and self-worth. These subtypes roughly coincide with Freud's exemplification of two fundamental mechanisms in depression, but there are also grounds for claiming that from both a developmental and a clinical perspective Blatt's subtypes of Anaclitic (dependent) and an Introjective (self-critical) depression have a lot in common with Klein's subtypes of paranoid-schizoid and depressive position depression.

From the point of view of the DSM-IV, what correlations or comparisons can be made with these psychoanalytic subtypes? Here we may be pursuing a false horizon. First, Freud's neurotic and narcissistic depressions are not two categories but two depressive processes that are distinguished qualitatively and include the factor of how mania as a dimension can saturate the clinical picture. Neurotic depression, though, is ranked as a milder form of depression psychoanalytically speaking, and in the DSM-III it was included in dysthymic disorder. In the DSM-IV, however, we find that neurotic depression is represented as major depressive disorder (MDD). In the ICD-10, neurotic depression was excluded and substituted with dysthymia, recurrent depression and depressive episode in terms of frequency. One persistent controversy surrounding the DSM-IV categories touches on their validity when there appears to be overlapping symptoms in the major categories. The exception is a higher loading of vegetative symptoms in MDD and the degree of severity of the symptoms. In terms of correlation, this would make MDD the more 'acute' disorder which is in line with my characterization of paranoid-schizoid depression as a narcissistic depression with predominantly vegetative symptoms owing to their originating in earlier and therefore deeper layers of the mind.

To conclude, the consensus among psychoanalytic writers on depression is in favour of two broad subtypes that can generate a small but significant number of dynamic pathways to depression. This is the conclusion reached by Bleichmar (1996) in his masterly review of a comprehensive basket of formulations by psychoanalysts down the years on the aetiology and dynamics of depression. His goals were twofold: to set about devising an integrative clinical model that could accommodate their common and diverse pathways and to demonstrate the importance of the correct treatment emphasis for any given subtype of depression. Overall, he nominates two major subtypes of depressions – 'narcissistic depression' and 'guilty depression'. He chooses aggression, in its varying forms, as the starting point for both depressions from which he adduces eight aetiological pathways to narcissistic depression and two pathways to guilty depression. Since it is impossible to accurately summarize all the perceptive details of his review I have included his visual flowchart of his summary and conclusions. In this chart we see just how integrative Bleichmar's model is in its characterization of multiple pathways to depression, which includes the external world. He may begin, perhaps controversially, with aggression as a starting point but the pathways he draws can accommodate many well-known aetiologies in depression unrelated to aggression.

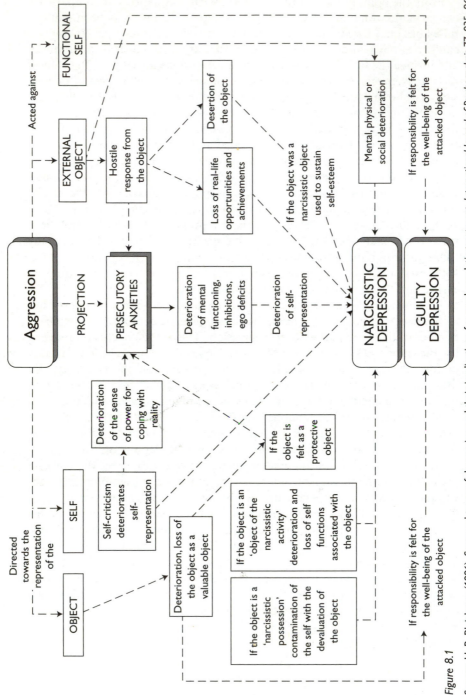

Figure 8.1

Source: H. B. Bleichmar (1996). Some subtypes of depression and their implications for psychoanalytic treatment. *International Journal of Psychoanalysis* 77, 935–961. Reproduced by permission of the publishers, Wiley-Blackwell, Oxford.

Chapter 9

A theoretical contribution to the problem of relapse

> Melancholy and mania, although treated in many medical books separately, are one and the same illness, and only differ according to the various grades of activity and diversity of affective states that occur in both.
>
> Andrés Piquer, physician to King Ferdinand VI of Spain

In Chapter 1 of this book I suggested that a return to theory might provide an opportunity to shed some additional light on the gloomy impression nowadays that most depressions are refractory and prognostically susceptible to relapse. In this chapter the phenomenon of relapse will be explored within an object relations framework. The intention is to show that a certain long-standing strand of thinking within psychoanalytic theory may allow for a different conceptualization of the structure of depression that, in turn, may provide some new thoughts on the apparent intractability of the disorder, as reflected in the high prevalence of relapse so frequently documented in the research and the clinical literature. This structure, incidentally, was pre-eminent in how the early pioneers in psychoanalysis approached depression: they always took notice of the interrelationship between depression and mania.

When Freud (1917) discussed melancholia in the context of mourning, he illustrated the importance of an in-depth understanding of healthy mental development to the clinical classification of mental disorders. A melancholic depression, he claimed, is distinguished by the subject's use of a mechanism that is developmentally prior to the one used by the mourner; that is, the mechanism of identification of a narcissistic type in place of an identification of an introjective type. Yet when he turned to the relationship between melancholia and mania, he was at first unable to find an association to anything in the normal mind regarding mania. Abraham (1924) supplied the link by pointing out that as the mourner completes the work of mourning, ordinarily there is an interval where sexual vitality returns and which leaves its stamp on renewed enthusiasms for work, relationships and play. This reabsorption of the outside world with exuberance, he explained, represents the 'mania' found in the recovery from normal or mild depression. In clinical mania or hypomania the same impulse takes the form of an indiscriminate and exalted absorption (and expulsion) of the world in all its scintillating forms. Further, to clarify why an attack on mania may occur on its own, that is, without a predisposing depression, Abraham (1924, p. 475) proposed the idea of a 'primal parathymia' to indicate that the conditions for mania could be met in early mental development when certain developmental tasks were not overcome. He also suggested that therapeutically the clinician should take full advantage of the intervals between depression and mania to introduce treatment, with the goal of neutralizing the cyclical process (Abraham 1924, p. 476). These statements, especially the proposal of an infantile prototype of depression, were made by Abraham with characteristic restraint – and with due deference to Freud – but being a psychiatrist, and following Kraepelin's axiom, his point was that a developmental line for depression should naturally include mania.

Melanie Klein (1940) went on to refine this genetic concept of 'infantile depressive illness' as a normal developmental phenomenon with its roots in the evolution of psychic structures in the average infant. The core developmental agenda for this 'illness', she indicated, is the transformation of narcissism into object love, which if unsuccessful, predisposes the adolescent and mature person to future depression, based not on observable symptoms alone but on deficits and imbalances in mental functioning. Like Abraham, she too envisaged a more interdependent relationship metapsychologically between obsessive, melancholic and manic states in depression. Based on her work with small children she developed the concept of a primary 'manic defence' to account for certain failures in overcoming a variety of schizoid and depressive anxieties and conflicts inherent in psychological growth. She pointed out: 'Fluctuations between the depressive and manic position are an essential part of normal development' (Klein 1940, p. 349). Where manic defences falter, she added, the ego introduces obsessional mechanisms to control or modify anxieties concerning separation and loss. These key elements became the hallmark of her theory of depression that, analogous to Abraham's conception, could be described as a revised theory of cyclothymic states.

The conceptualization that can be inferred from these statements is that the psychopathology of depression and its structure is better understood as a disorder of mood intimately related to mania. That is, it is necessary to view all depressions – healthy, mild or severe – as essentially unipolar depressions, but they can be conceptualized as having a cyclothymic structure in the sense that circular activity between depressed and manic states, varying in periodicity and intensity, can be viewed as an intrinsic feature of their morphology. This conceptualization stretches back to Kraepelin (1902, 1921) and the early psychoanalytic pioneers who placed mania and depression under the same umbrella and viewed them not as discrete conditions, nor as polar opposites, but as one illness. It is this link between depression and mania, I believe, that comprises the hidden structure of depression when appraised from an object relations standpoint.

The implication of this conceptualization is that mania and depression always exist in a living cohabitative relationship – depression relies on the speeding-up aspect of mania or hypomania to minimize some of its intolerable effects, especially upon the body, while mania takes advantage of the slowing-down aspect of depression to usurp control of the faculty of judgement. In other words, manic states are an integral and complementary part of the depressive process in which the psychological work necessary for the recovery from depression can be interrupted, or foreclosed, in an organized way through the contra-depressive effect of mania. Accordingly, except in extreme cases, there is no morphological variance between depression and mania – they exist interdependently. This implies emphatically that the interrelationship is not a bi-polar one, but a cyclical one.

Hence, the notion of 'manic defence', so eloquently described by Winnicott (1935) as 'the notorious holiday from depression'. It may be added that manic defences comprise a number of avoidant thoughts, fantasies and behaviours that are not always evident in the presenting clinical picture. They emerge manifestly in a longer interview or treatment situation with practitioners attuned to unconscious factors, confirming the long-standing belief among psychoanalytic clinicians that, intrinsically, depression is a complex dimensional disorder.

Both Winnicott (1935) and Klein (1940) described manic defences as a class of mental operations based in denial. In depression, this denial can draw the patient in one of two directions – towards an oral idealization of external reality or an oral fixation of inner reality, both of which create a form of psychic numbing that can with great precision be mobilized to nullify the painful affects of depression. The 'flight' to external reality is characterized by fantasies that rapidly replace one another and by the incitement to action. The 'flight' to inner reality is distinguished by states of dissociation, depersonalization and misperceptions reflecting an insidious impairment to the general contact with external reality. This is essentially a clinical theory framed within an object relations paradigm and derived from analytic work across all ages, over many years, and culminating in a classification of this special class of defences. They include, first, self-idealization, second, denial and devaluation of the significance of needed objects, third, omnipotent phantasies of being superior and in control of these objects, and fourth, getting the better of these objects in a state of triumph. Manic defences are common to everyone regardless of stage of development but in some adults they have crystallized into a characterological defence; however, for the purposes of this discussion no distinction will be made between the two.

The suggestion in this chapter is that when all depressions are viewed conceptually as unipolar depressions with a core cyclothymic structure, this may permit a different analysis and discussion about the dynamics of relapse. The second suggestion is that where the excessive deployment of manic defences interferes with an adequate recovery phase in depression this sets in motion conditions favourable for chronicity and relapse. It was Freud (1921) who wrote that the cyclical depressions have psychogenic origins, hence the conditions for relapse can be theorized to have its origins in the depressive process itself – it is an 'inside job', so to speak. *Moreover, it is precisely this cyclical structure that predisposes depression to chronicity and recurrence.* Therefore, an adequate recovery depends on coming to grips with the range and influence of manic defences that strategically should be elevated to one of the primary foci of treatment. Put simply, the mechanisms of the denial of depression, especially where they take the form of unconscious denial, should be kept in mind by the clinician in conjunction with the manifest suffering of the patient. It follows that if treatment is simply concerned with the improvement of symptoms, or symptomatic thinking, then a powerful factor in relapse is overlooked.

This thesis is set out with great distinction by Goodwin and Jamison (2007) from which the quotation that begins this chapter is taken. Proceeding from a historical perspective these authors bemoan the fact that successive DSMs have destroyed any concept of a unipolar depression with cyclical features (Goodwin and Jamison 2007, p. 9) and they emphasize that this development has eliminated an important variable in understanding the phenomenon of recurrence. While their particular focus is on recurrence, this chapter limits itself to the thorny question of relapse in the context of contemporary treatment outcomes in trials. In that sense, however, there is agreement in recognizing the merit of a fundamental cyclothymic structure to depression that involves circular states of depression countered by manic defences that stands in opposition to DSM philosophy of discrete descriptive categories. While no one can deny that this system has brought reliability and validity of diagnosis to the field of mental illness generally, the successful treatment of depression, by contrast, has been retarded due to a linear (bi-polar) and somewhat over-simplified model of mood disorders.[1]

The case of adolescent depression is interesting and may be illustrative. When the treatment of adolescent depression with SSRIs was introduced a significant number of patients succumbed to induced mania (Chang and Ketter 2001). It was presumed that since depression was the presenting symptom it was likely that these adolescents were experiencing an initial bi-polar episode. This led to cautionary warnings in using these medications with youngsters without a mood stabilizer – regarded nowadays as axiomatic in the pharmacological treatment of bi-polar adolescents. Such a conclusion, however, while inadvertently lending some support to the claim of this chapter – that a cyclothymic structure exists as a core of depression

– nonetheless neglects to discuss the iatrogenic factor of medication. Instead, the anomalous clinical problem is simply solved by fitting the adolescent into a Procrustean bed of a double pharmacological intervention. Subsequent studies have reinforced the high risk of SSRI-induced mania among paediatric patients (Baumer et al. 2006).

A simpler approach, reflecting a simple truth, would be to recognize that adolescence is a peak time for the appearance of cyclothymic states and that apart from hormonal contributions they are prompted by one of the primary tasks of this maturational phase – an emotional disengagement from the internalized object relations of childhood in the service of individuation. In such a case any cautionary warnings concerning the treatment of depressed adolescents would emphasize the *expectation* of manic defences, and the necessity of highlighting or targeting their mood cycling effects. In other words, at peak times in the maturational processes the cyclothymic structure of depression is heightened as are the strategies to deny depression through the mobilization of a manic defence.[2]

Implications for treatment

As mentioned in Chapter 1, it is difficult to avoid the conclusion, given the statistics on relapse, that customary treatment regimes have made little impact on some core aspect of the anatomy of depression that, so far, has resisted the powers of clinical research trials to demonstrate long-term benefit. A question was also raised about these treatments, and what part, if any, they have played in today's discouraging landscape on treatment outcome. The most widely tested treatments for efficacy in depression are the structured brief treatments such as CBT, IPT or brief dynamic psychotherapy, and, of course, antidepressant medication.

I wonder if brief treatment regimes, of whatever theoretical orientation or clinical philosophy, while achieving good early rates of remission, also mobilize manic defences in the patient with the effect that only a partial remission is achieved during the structured treatment interval. Such treatments show patients getting well over 16 weeks but if no recognition is given to the patient's aptitude for the denial of depression, *particularly* in the treatment context, then this may simply establish the conditions for temporary or pseudo-remission. In fact, this pseudo-remission is clearly evidenced in the frequent presence of residual symptoms following optimal treatment, symptoms that have long been recognized as a critical factor in relapse (Paykel 2008). This argument would suggest that the newly coined term of 'treatment-resistant depression' is something of a misnomer – since it is not the illness that is resistant but the depressed person who resists recovery through the use of certain natural defences to excess. It is therefore suggested that in order to address this question of the latent vulnerability to relapse inherent in the activation of manic defences, a far greater vigilance is necessary during the assessment period and beyond, and that greater care should be given to the design, structure and goals of therapy.

That the proponents of brief forms of therapy are no less concerned about relapse rates is indicated by increasing recommendations in that community for 'booster' therapy or extended forms of therapy following optimal treatment, as a safeguard against regression (Beck et al. 2004). In addition, considerable attention has been given to patients with 'depressive interlock', that is, those patients who are at risk of relapse or recurrence due to a continued presence of 'depresso-typic' cognitive structuring (Teasdale et al. 1995). I would suggest that manic defences are a central but hidden feature of such structuring.

The requirement of add-on treatment has also become the view in the pharmacological treatment of depression, notwithstanding ample concerns about habituation and the long-term side-effects on the central nervous system (Martin et al. 2004). So, there does appear to be some recognition of the fact that an important therapeutic task is not adequately fulfilled by these treatments, yet what that task is, is obviously open to interpretation. In the case of medication, 'more of the same' or adjusting the choice of medication is a customary solution, but it has become increasingly doubtful that by itself – that is, without sequential therapy, usually CBT – that such a strategy will achieve an improved long-term prognosis in terms of pre-venting recurrence (Peterson 2006).

Longer-term CBT has its own challenges. It has been well established empirically that a positive treatment alliance is a significant factor in the successful psychological treatment of depression, regardless of treatment length or clinical philosophy. An emphasis on the 'positive' nevertheless may preclude clinical attention to the patient's negative attitudes towards the therapist, as well as towards the chosen process of therapy itself – a factor that plausibly exists alongside the patient's desire to feel better and to be more resilient. It seems inescapable that the longer the treatment pro-gramme, the more likely complex interpersonal factors will filter into the therapeutic process and that the more demand there will be for an inter-pretative stance. Such a development would be evidenced in the way the patient's *unconscious* beliefs about depression, and its meaning, become part of the therapeutic context; hence, in terms of treatment philosophy these factors may need to be accommodated in any theoretical system that makes claims about the causal link between conscious depressive thoughts or beliefs and depressed mood.[3]

The phenomena of unconscious beliefs is more familiar to clinicians who situate the manic defences at the centre of their thinking about depression, especially in its complex and refractory forms. However, not all theoretical models within psychoanalysis subscribe to these concepts derived from object relations theories. The *Psychodynamic Diagnostic Manual* (PDM Task Force 2006), for instance, in its discussion of depression contains only two fleeting references to the defensive role of mania in depression (pp. 46 and 47). This pioneering manual was the result of a collaboration between five major organizations representing psychoanalytically oriented mental health professionals in the United States, and its laudable intention was to provide a complementary diagnostic classification of mental functioning to the DSM. However, the stated goal by the authors of creating a system sympathetic and appropriate to the complexity, as opposed to the testability, of the phenomena in the psychoanalytic field may have been compromised by a preference for particular theories and concepts while ignoring others. For example, it is remarkable that in major chapters on child and adolescent symptom patterns and the classification of disorders in infancy and early childhood, there is not one mention given of Winnicott.

To conclude, it has been argued that by returning to the interrelationship between depression and mania as theorized by the early pioneers and by subsequent generations of psychoanalysts, with special attention to those representing the British Object Relations school, a contribution can be made to understanding why positive outcomes in clinical trials utilizing some forms of brief therapy for depression are not consistently or robustly reproduced outside treatment. (See pioneers such as Radó (1928), Deutsch (1933), Weiss (1944), Fenichel (1945), Jacobson (1953) and Rochlin (1953).) The suggestion is that all depressions should be conceptualized as having a cyclothymic structure in which circular activity between depressed and manic states are intrinsic to their morphology. Time and time again in the analytic treatment situation this is illustrated in the oscillations in the patient between anxiety, depressed and manic states. Mixed-state depressions therefore should not be regarded as a subtype of depression but as the norm, as Emil Kraepelin (1921) had originally recognized, based on a patient-centred approach. This viewpoint essentially describes the state of internal object relations in depression that evinces the unconscious structure of depression.

The deployment of manic defences – Freud called them 'periodic rebellions' – are therefore ever present in the clinical picture as sub-threshold features, and when activated they impede the adequate recovery phase and set in motion certain mental conditions for recycling and relapse. This can lead to an erroneous diagnosis of bi-polar depression. Worse still, if that diagnosis is treated with antidepressants alone this produces the iatrogenic effect of rapid cycling and to a higher incidence of recurrence (Schneck et al. 2008). Such circular activity between defensive mania and depression is precisely what prevents the suffering of the depressive being brought to an end.

Furthermore, it is contended that manualized brief treatments, of whatever theoretical orientation or clinical philosophy, naturally mobilize manic defences that if disregarded can contribute to a type of pseudo-remission that is not sustainable over time.

Finally, it is alleged that the overriding need to achieve consistency in the description of depression and to estimate treatment empirically has led to an oversimplified concept of depression that has had a direct bearing on the current pessimistic view about the realizable goals of treatment. By reconceptualizing depression, and by including all the major defences against depression in the clinical philosophy and technical interventions of therapy, it is possible that the current 'impasse of therapeutic nihilism' – as Abraham (1911) once famously described the psychiatric attitude to manic depression – may give way to a more favourable though no less complex outlook on treatment possibilities.

Chapter 10

The correlation between dream work and the work of mourning

A patient Steven, a 17-year-old completing his final year at school, was referred for help in dealing with the abrupt death of an older brother. His 20-year-old brother, Rick, who had been a student living in digs at the time, was hit by a car while crossing an intersection. Family members including Steven rushed to the scene and found Rick conscious. An ambulance arrived and while other members went with Rick to the hospital, Steven and an uncle remained at the scene to deal with police statements. Shortly after his arrival at the hospital, however, Rick slipped into a coma and lived for a few weeks before his death. Steven was very upset that he didn't get the opportunity of saying goodbye.

During the assessment meeting I was impressed with Steven's honesty and fortitude in coming to terms with his loss. However, even though he spoke thoughtfully, he appeared unemotional when describing events. He was very engaging but he seemed on edge and at the same time quite flat, whereas in contrast I felt tearful listening to his account of these awful events.

Then he mentioned a number of symptoms: his troubled sleep, a throbbing pain in his side and his difficulties in concentrating in class and on the rugby field. The family GP had diagnosed depression but Steven was implacably against medication. To my surprise he next recounted a dream, the content of which left me feeling more hopeful as it suggested that his unconscious had begun the work of mourning. We began once-a-week time-limited (to nine months) therapy as Steven was planning on travelling overseas following his final exams.

What I propose to do in this chapter is to present Steven's dreams which, with one exception, formed a complete sequence over the nine months of his sessions. This sequence, I believe, illustrates what has been long established by clinical psychoanalysis – that dreaming of a lost one tends to draw out the most intense pain and grief experienced during the period of mourning, particularly in accepting the reality of the loss. That is to say, that the work of mourning deploys the dream, in a unique way, for the purposes of processing grief. In addition, however, I came to recognize that the actual content of Steven's dreams as they concerned his dead brother – taken as a continuous narrative of images and events – also personified the transformational work that is the goal of mourning. In other words, the chronological content and narrative of the dreams depicted the actual psychic restoration process by which the dead person is established in the ego via introjective identification. This depiction was one in which an initially fragile, unwell, broken older brother figure was, by degrees, brought back to wholeness, aliveness, and reasonable health resembling his condition at the time of his death. It is in this manner that the chronological dream content mirrored the 'work of mourning'. I would like to discuss this interesting phenomenon even though it may be a familiar observation to many clinicians who have presided over a mourning process of this kind. The individual dreams will be given first, in sequence, followed by Steven's associations and emotional responses and will include some piecing together comments by the therapist. A discussion of Hanna Segal's (1991) ideas on the link between the work of mourning and the psychic work that produces a dream – the dream work – will follow.

Steven's dreams in sequence

1. I'm driving through a twilight city landscape which has a science fiction feel. It's a convertible car that seems to be driving itself. Rick is in the passenger seat with his head on my lap. He's weak and wordless and much younger (cries) but his eyes are open and he's alive and I stop the car. A roughly dressed priest smoking a cigarette leans over him and puts the cigarette in his mouth. It's a Camel light – and I light it and he seems to improve. Then he turns his head and looks around and finds a packet of cigs underneath the seat. Then we are in a restaurant and a waiter appears carrying a candle with a huge flame (cries).

Comment

Steven spoke of finding cigarettes in Rick's bag at the accident scene and of smoking them. He agreed when I suggested that he had loved his brother as if he was a 'huge flame' that had suddenly gone out. He spontaneously added that he had been avoiding his girlfriend all week because he felt numbed – the flame had gone out there too. Steven responded well to my asking for further associations. He confessed to driving a car without a licence and to smoking, sometimes sharing a cigarette with his brother, without his parents' knowledge. It seems that the dream tries to disguise Steven's guilt in a number of ways – by letting the car (a convertible and therefore a more dangerous car) drive itself, and by denying the health risks of smoking by the projection of guilt onto the 'cool' priest who, by association, turns out to be the biological father who left the family when the boys were younger – in other words, a reference to a previous loss.

> 2. I'm standing with Rick on a slope of a hill (where we lived as children). Rick had a bag slung over his shoulder and was restless. He wanted to get into a car but I was delaying things. Then he's driving me up Station Road. He was younger in the dream and I said emotionally, 'I am so pleased to see you, you died!' He laughed and looked at me. He was so *real* and I said to myself, 'Can I be dreaming?' I convinced myself in the dream that he was alive and I was so pleased. Then as I woke up I felt a sinking feeling when I realized I'd been dreaming. I was amazed in the dream how vivid and alive he was. Actually, at the moment (Steven added), I find I'm struggling to see him vividly in my mind (cries).

Comment

The dream as a 'vehicle' for the work of mourning is well illustrated here. Rick is on the move and his presence is absolutely vivid and intense, yet there is doubt about whether this is real. Steven hesitates about going in the car because of its obvious association with danger. He tries his best to mentally hold onto Rick, but on waking the truth is laid bare. There is pain in waking life too where Steven worries about forgetting his brother.

> 3. A weird man came to visit me – a lanky, at ease, working-class guy in his 40s, slightly rough looking. He appeared with some black labourers who were in blue overalls like they were movers. We were talking about the man's work and then Rick was with me, and then we were in bed and this man came to kiss me on the head and he lit my cigarette and then left. I said, 'Look at this guy – he's got a tow-truck.' Then I was aware of Rick's presence and I convinced myself that he was really alive and that what had come before was just a dream. He asked me how he had died and I said, 'From internal injuries'. 'Where?' he asked. 'In Egypt,' I replied, which woke me up and I wrote the dream down feeling very upset. Steven recollected that while on a school trip to the Middle East he had sent Rick a postcard depicting two statues in the Valley of the Kings, sitting rigidly. In the card he was trying to wind Rick up by saying, 'I thought you'd like the rigidity of these figures.' (Cries bitterly.)

Comment

The man in the dream was again confirmed as the father who was lost to both boys in their youth – he is returning as a memory of someone who once tucked the boys in, but also as a wished-for fatherly rescuer (tow-truck) in the present circumstances. A transference factor, that was not interpreted, was enhanced by the fact that some work was being done on the road outside the therapist's consulting room. Again there is guilt over having called his brother 'rigid', which must be an unconscious pun of being dead. The return of the father in the dream illustrates Klein's point, namely, that in recovering from loss by reinstating the lost object you are not doing so for the first time. In addition, the recovery of a specific lost object via introjective identification involves a recovery of a circle of internal objects that originally existed in childhood.

> 4. I am in a hospital with Rick. He wakes up from a coma and says he's not feeling well. I feel strongly protective of him. One of his ex-girlfriends appears and I tell her to go away. Then I'm in a restaurant with Rick and he's not feeling well and wants to sleep in the car. He's groggy and I need to reorientate him. He was younger, a teenager like me, I suppose.

Comment

In the session Steven mentions that all week he has been feeling 'misty' in his head yet he is simultaneously feeling more 'connected' to Rick. He mentions Rick's ex-girlfriend whom he has always had a crush on. He admits he might be developing a strong attraction to this young woman, who keeps visiting the family house. In the dream Rick wakes up from a coma (as if he has only been asleep) and says he's not feeling well. Then in the restaurant he has to leave and lie down in the car. He's 'groggy' as if he's only intoxicated and he is younger, a teenager 'like me', says Steven. There are three attempts to deny loss in the dream: the wish for Rick to have survived his coma; the connection to Rick via the similarity between Rick's 'grogginess' and Steven's 'misty' head; and the wish to take his brother's place with his girlfriend disguised as over-protectiveness. All three are examples of feeling more 'connected' to Rick and seem to be based on an identification by projection that secures a narcissistic merger with the object as a defence against loss.

> 5. I went home and asked my mother how Rick was and she said that he was struggling to walk. He was lying down on the couch and he raised his head to see me and lay down again. We talked about his cough and mother said he was going to see Dr C. Then I woke up and was shocked to realize he was dead.

Comment

In the session Steven spoke of wanting to 'leave this world' – of going to live in Europe after completing school. He didn't feel at home in his hometown any more, he didn't feel safe either. 'Ontologically', he said, 'it's unpredictable.' And he couldn't see value in anything local. I took up his feeling of hopelessness in bringing his brother back and how he might prefer to leave the country and the world too as Rick had done. I checked whether he had any thoughts of dying, which he denied. Note how in acute grief the state of the entire internal world is affected – 'ontologically'.

> 6. I was coming home and walking through the door. I was looking for the light switch. Suddenly a dog burst through the kitchen door, like Rick's old dog. Then Rick came in looking tired and he sat down at the table with his back to me. I joined him and he was slumped with his eyes closed and I realized something was wrong. He lifted his hand and put it into my mouth and closed his eyes, as if he was saying goodbye to me. I started making animal sounds, whimpering, soothing sounds. It occurred to me he was dying and I was overcome with sadness, and woke up crying.

Comment

Steven said he thought that in the dream he was acknowledging his brother's death for the first time. I asked, 'How?' He answered that Rick had come to visit to say goodbye. He added that he had been feeling worse since the dream and had not been able to get to sleep again. The dog in the dream, Steven confirmed, was a family dog that had died years before (another previous loss returned to). When the dog had died, Rick was overseas (cries). I commented that on that occasion he had been alone in saying goodbye to the dog – as he now felt about having to say goodbye to Rick. In this dream the lively dog seems to represent a previously lively Rick, who now in the dream is weak and dying. Furthermore, the appearance of the dog represents something they once shared but would no longer be able to share – a hint of resignation.

> 7. An old friend of mine from primary school, whose brother also died some time ago, called me to tell me he'd seen Rick in another city. I tried to correct him and said, 'But he died!' Then suddenly I was in a room with a window to one side overlooking a terrace. Someone darted past the window and then sneaked back under the windowsill. I went out and it was Rick. He was his current age, slightly bloated, but he said he'd come out of hospital. He was kidding around and I was so pleased to see him, but all the time I knew his presence could not be true.

Comment

On this occasion it is someone else who has sighted Rick in another city and Steven has to correct him by telling him Rick has died. In the dream Steven has apparently accepted the reality of his loss. Then the dream suddenly presents Rick at his present age, but retaining his youthfulness, as reflected in the hide-and-seek game with his brother. This dream sorely tests Steven's work of mourning but touchingly he admits, 'I was so pleased to see him but all the time I knew his presence could not be true' – another sign of resignation. Steven mentions in the session he has reached the high point of his sadness.

> 8. Steven dreamt Rick was talking to him about his ex-girlfriend. Rick said, 'Regretfully I'm taking her back'. Steven stated that he realized in the dream that she wasn't really interested in him. He reported, 'So, begrudgingly I accepted that Rick had more of a right to her than me.'

Comment

In this dream Rick claims his ex-girlfriend back and this indicates a greater degree of separateness between the brothers. During the course of his mourning Steven had fallen in love with this ex-girlfriend, as a means of stepping into Rick's shoes, but in the dream we see evidence of a lessening of his narcissistic identification with Rick as a means of holding onto him.

> 9. I dreamt my brother was leaving a message on his answerphone talking about his feelings. I cried in the dream and woke up feeling that he was a part of me again.

> 10. My new girlfriend (in the future) and I were going to buy a house in the country. Not an expensive house and one in need of renovation. Rick phoned and suggested he could go and live there for a while and start the renovation. He said he would like to live in the country for a year and be creative and reflective.

Discussion

Following a period of shock and disbelief – and protest – the mourner in waking life attempts to recover the object in thought, memory and also through active seeking, only to discover that the lost loved one is nowhere to be found. Freud called this the period of 'reality testing' that he situated at the heart of the work of mourning. I believe Steven's dreams provide a veritable crucible for this aspect of the work of mourning and I would like to emphasize how this occurs on two levels. First, the dreams face him with the universal shock of loss by emphasizing so starkly and bleakly the difference between fantasy and reality. In fact, Steven's dreams exemplify the work of mourning by going backwards and forwards to the terrible event, at once accepting his loss and then clambering back and away from it. Rick consistently appears alive in his dreams, though ill or damaged or struggling, and this serves to intensify Steven's attachment to him, only to be faced dream after dream with all the reasons why he has to give up his attachment. This is an example of how the work of mourning, in a unique way, deploys the dream for the purposes of processing grief.

Yet, second, the dreams also reveal something interesting about the process by which the dead person is transformed in the mourner's unconscious as part of the work of mourning. At the beginning of the dream sequence, Rick is in a very weak state and barely alive. He is also younger in these dreams, harking back to healthier childhood times. However, as the dreams proceed chronologically we see a transformation of the dead person from a weaker, damaged younger figure into a more ambulatory figure, then into a more restored figure closer in age, health and personality to the time when he died.[1] This type of transformation plainly reflects the stages necessary for the release of the object from reality in order for it to be installed in the ego as a living internal object.

I believe the dreams also depict this actual process – Steven's gradual resuscitation of Rick in his dreams is in direct proportion to his progressive letting go of Rick, little by little, until he reaches a state of final resignation. In other words, the narrative of the chronological sequence of dreams mirrored the very task of mourning: as Rick became more of a third party in Steven's dreams, talking to and referring to others, being reported on by others, taking his girlfriend back, leaving messages on Steven's answer-phone, he became more separated out as a person in Steven's mind, and this separation reflected a shift in the status of the lost object from a narcissistic object (reflecting the operation of a narcissistic identification) to an internal object (reflecting the operation of an introjective identification). The last dream, significantly, finds Rick in a sufficiently revived state in Steven's mind that he is capable of volunteering his help with the internal and external renovation of his brother's own life as he moves towards the future. It can be inferred from this compelling example that the dream work can play an imperative role in directing the work of mourning.

In her writings on symbolism Segal (1991) has often spoken of a link between the psychic work undertaken during mourning and the psychic work that produces a dream – the dream work. The link, she has suggested, is unconscious symbolization. Freud (1900) eschewed all ideas that the function of the dream work was anything other than distortional, with no creative potential whatsoever. Departing from this position, Segal distinguishes between the conscious symbol that might appear in a dream and unconscious symbolization that she describes as a transformational process that has features in common with the mourning process. She sees the parallel between the work of mourning and dream work as follows: in the work of mourning the actual dead person cannot be brought to life except symbolically, and this constitutes a significant criteria for successful mourning (Segal 1991, p. 38). In dreams, the dream work converts the latent thoughts into disguised contents through mechanisms such as condensation and displacement – including unconscious symbolisation. Thus, concludes Segal, both the work of mourning and dream work can be considered examples of 'working through', and this is especially the case when the dream emanates from some aspect of the transference.

I have chosen this series of dreams in a young man, in response to the sudden and violent loss of his brother, to illustrate the homology described by Segal (1991) between the process of dream work and the process of the work of mourning. This can be summarized thus: in the dream work the manifest content is given a new form by the latent content while in the work of mourning the lost object is given the new form of an internal object. The process they seem to share in common is the process of symbolisation that could be claimed to be continuous activity that occurs in waking life as unconscious phantasy and during sleep as dreams (Bion 1962). With this case presentation, however, I have tried to add another dimension to this homology: that the narrative content of dreams in the mourner as they concern the lost object not only depicts the transformational structure and dynamics of the work of mourning, but also appears to *direct* this process. This adds another interesting component to the manner in which the work of mourning deploys the dream for the purposes of processing grief. It also leads us to consider a wider transformational function of dreams in the maturational processes generally, as it reflects stages of mental and emotional development (Bion 1965; Meltzer 1984).

In concluding this chapter I would like to highlight how the patient in mourning ineluctably returns to his or her past relationship with the lost object, as well as automatically revisits other past losses or lost objects. This is an integral aspect of the mourning 'process' as Klein (1940) and others have described it. Oddly, it has been known for some detractors of the analytic therapies, particularly those in the biomedical field, to profess that in treating depression related to loss there is no point in delving into the patient's past. 'The point is that we know how to treat [depression]; philosophising where it comes from has not so far been of the slightest therapeutic usefulness' (Donald Klein, quoted in Solomon 2002, p. 103). The bizarre implication of this statement is that a depressive response to loss – including unforeseen responses – is something foreign imposed on the patient by psychotherapy that will interfere with the recovery process.

Chapter 11

Case study

A type of identification found in depression-related loss

On referral, Mrs. D, a young married woman, was concerned about feeling 'frozen' inside and having lost, over several months – perhaps even for a year – her enthusiasm for a number of her usual activities like reading, socializing and taking weekend trips to the countryside. She said that her 'emotional repertoire' had dwindled to the point where at dinner parties she felt stifled and with less and less to say. She also mentioned feeling tearful a lot, and of struggling with confidence at work, where she occupied a very senior position. When I mentioned the word 'depression' Mrs. D responded by looking quite drowsy and she commented that my using that word had triggered something. In passing, towards the end of the session she made mention of the death of her mother twenty years ago, who had died at the age of 50 from brain cancer.

While Mrs. D began her twice-weekly treatment focusing on current issues in her life such as the waning of intimacy with her husband, her complex but mainly resentful relationship with her employer and her sense of persecution by an indifferent father, in the course of the next four months the circumstances and emotional climate surrounding her mother's illness and death trickled into the foreground. Following a diagnosis of a brain tumour an operation was unsuccessful and her mother was confined to bed in the family home, where she gradually faded away. Mrs. D, a young unmarried woman at the time, returned home to nurse her mother and to attend to visitors who called on a daily basis. When her mother died she was in a coma. In the last stages of her life, her mother would suddenly become lucid and say something heart-rending – Mrs. D felt totally helpless. Throughout this period her father, a polite yet oversensitive man, not given to excess of any kind, carried on with his life as normal, returning from work in the evenings and going to bed. He had offered Mrs. D no comfort at all during the three months she attended to her mother, and to him. When her mother died, there was 'no drama'. At the funeral none of her mother's friends or family members were asked to give an oration and in spite of her mother's lifelong interest in music, none was allowed. Her father then disposed of her mother's possessions in a peremptory and insensitive way; within a year he had sold the family home and moved to another town. In mentioning this detail Mrs. D became acutely distressed, saying, 'My mother would never have left a child!'

As her therapy progressed, Mrs. D's unhappiness with her father's behaviour smouldered into anger, but she could not conceive of any way of talking to him about it. She realized that this was in line with the family doctrine of 'keeping up appearances'. Recently her mother's birthday had come and gone without a comment from her father. She said that since childhood she had always felt like something 'patched onto' his life.

After three months in therapy Mrs. D had recovered some of her zest owing to some intimacy having returned to the marital relationship; however she also began to be plagued by bleak thoughts. In one session she asked, 'How long will this depression last?' This question unexpectedly triggered a more acute phase of suffering marked by a foggy brain, heavy eyelids and near physical immobilization. In tandem, the terrible mental struggle of feeling worse – yet having to keep up appearances – reached its zenith. She had one erotic dream that involved a sexual interaction with a much older male friend that left her totally perplexed. I understood this dream to be a manic defence against her statement 'How long will this depression last?' that I took to be a reference to the period of three months she had spent presiding over her mother's gradual death.

The work of mourning mobilizes depression and my intention in this chapter is to illustrate how in the case of delayed mourning depression takes an acute and complex form. I will begin by detailing the fluctuations in Mrs. D's symptoms over this period of maximal depression that spanned the next three months and will offer a formulation of the nature of her depression from a psychodynamic viewpoint. I will also describe what I understood as three phases of her grief in which her depression took different forms. First, an acute period marked by a reliving of her mother's death where her depression had strong narcissistic features expressed through states of depersonalization, but accompanied by partial remission of symptoms. In the second phase neurotic features of her depression came to the fore that were associated with the recall of conflictual experiences with her mother and with Oedipal jealousy. This was followed by a longer phase with a circular pattern where periods of intense symptoms alternated with intervals of relief and a return of normal mood and functioning – this represented a phase of 'working though' in the transference.

Phase of maximal depression

Mrs. D came in and said she felt wretched. She couldn't stop crying since the last session. She had felt so sad and unable to do anything. She couldn't read, she had tried a walk but that didn't help. She cried in the shower. She said, 'Everything to do with solitude brings it on'. So, she decided to put herself to bed and when she turned the light out she found herself crying in the dark. While crying she remembered this was exactly what she had done during the period her mother was dying. At the time she had decided to sleep in the bedroom next door to her mother and each night she had cried herself to sleep. 'In my imagination,' she said, referring to the present, 'I became that person'. She added that she had also remembered many things she had forgotten. How, for example, during the day she had attended to visitors, making tea and sandwiches, and she realized how her father had kept out of the picture. In the evenings he would read the newspaper and retire to bed, leaving her alone with mother. She said with surprise and exasperation that all this had happened twenty years ago! How could she recall it so literally?

Then in the morning she woke up and spontaneously began cooking. She made fishcakes, with all the elaborate procedures necessary, and she commented on the smell that was so fresh. Then she made soup, but it was time to go to work. Her crying had stopped but she felt terrible and in a hideous place. In the session she suddenly exclaimed, 'I would have cooked for my mother too!' and she became very upset. I commented that she had remembered how she had coped in solitude with her grief. In response, she reiterated that it had felt exactly how it was at the time. That evening she returned home from work and didn't want to leave the house. She made excuses to her husband since she didn't want anyone to know how she was feeling. I said this was how it was at the time too – she couldn't go out and she couldn't talk to anyone about how she felt, particularly her father.

In the next session following the weekend Mrs. D recounted how 'permeable' she had become – there was nothing to shield her, no filter. 'I see a beggar on the streets and I feel tearful. I'm like a child.' Simultaneously, she also felt 'impermeable' to the world. She couldn't read, she wasn't hungry; she had no desire to talk, did not feel like getting up in the mornings and staggered through the day with no clarity or organization of thought. I commented that not having a filter was very difficult because this felt like she had no protection. She became tearful and said that at times during the day it was so hard to hold back on how she felt . . . and then it goes away! Was that normal? I commented that there was sadness in her tears because when her mother was dying, there was no mother to shield her from this awful experience. 'No father either', she added. Following a painful silence, Mrs. D then said that she had been to visit a friend over the weekend but had been exhausted by the experience. In driving home she had felt so tired in her mind that she could have gone off the road. I said that when she felt there was no one there to shield her, she couldn't keep her mind on the road. She looked up in surprise and commented that in the run-up to her mother going into hospital for her operation, she had had a few minor car accidents. I said that at the moment she was trying to stay in touch with her mother.

At the start of the next week, Mrs. D spoke of continuing on a rollercoaster. She said the cooking had come and gone and that now she felt nauseous in the presence of food. However, a memory of her mother had come back in the bathroom when she caught a whiff of a medical smell from her mother's bedside and that made her go in and out of tears for the morning. Then she decided to go ahead with a visit to an aunt and was introduced to someone as 'my sister's daughter'. She felt grateful, and because of family resemblance, she experienced this time with her aunt as having spent time with her mother. However, she could not mention anything to her aunt about her mother or how she was feeling. On her way home she felt 'dead tired', 'knocked out' and didn't know who she was. 'I thought I was losing it. We ran out of milk at home and I just couldn't be bothered. I tried reading but my brain couldn't hold a sentence. I'd rather be dead! Why am I alive when I'm like this!' I suggested that the visit to her aunt had got her close to her mother again; she had created some distance since the last session when the cooking came and went, but in getting closer through her aunt, she then had to leave and experience her loss all over again. I said I agreed – no one should be made to live like this. Mrs. D looked moved and struck by this. In her thoughtfulness she considered whether her mother might have actually felt like this – that she wanted to die. After a pause I agreed, and added that in her speaking the words, 'I'd rather be dead! Why am I alive when I'm like this!' Mrs. D was speaking her mother's thoughts but, of course, they had to remain unspoken thoughts. Mrs. D now became very tearful and replied, 'Because she couldn't leave me!'

In her following session Mrs. D said that some nerve had been hit in the last session as she had become raw for two days and found herself constantly on the verge of tears. She said she could not recall what had gone on in the session and had thrown a 'shroud' over herself at work, making herself absent. However, by that evening she recovered and in talking to her husband, she had realized what the meaning of the 'milk' was. When she once visited her father in his new home, there was no milk for her tea. He, of course, didn't take milk in his tea, and she felt this was typical of his indifference, in spite of knowing she was visiting. I said she was remembering again her sense of her father's absence in not giving her something vital at the time when her mother was dying – and following her death.

This prompted Mrs. D to produce a spurt of negative memories from childhood. Sunday afternoons were excruciating. There was no one to talk to, father read the newspaper or watched cricket and mother would be doing housework. So she buried herself in reading that became her passion. But she thought she was very lonely and unhappy. There was also a memory of her mother's slavish attitude towards her father, how she dropped everything for him so that he was never inconvenienced. She highlighted the example of Thursdays when the servants were off. Her mother (and herself) would deputize by opening the garden gate so that father could 'swoop' up the driveway into the garage with ease. She hated that part of her mother. She also mentioned her mother's over-involvement in her school and social activities and how 'devouring' this felt. 'She required so much informa-tion'. Of course, nothing could be said, hence she rebelled by 'winging' it and lying about doing her homework. She would also give her mother what she wanted without enthusiasm – it became a 'compulsion', she said. Sometimes she fobbed her off in discussions, knowing she was a keen conversationalist. I pointed out the sexual allusion in mother letting father swoop up the driveway into the garage and interpreted that her compulsive thwarting of her mother was therefore a punish-ment for her relationship with father. This anger with her parents must have intensified her sense of loneliness, I added.

Following these protests about her mother, Mrs. D returned to the next session (following a weekend) complaining that her concentration had been worse. She had felt emotionally tender following the last session and had grown anxious in a curious way – 'neurotic anxiety' she called it. Her jaw too had become clenched which she associated to pent-up feelings. She spoke about a work colleague who had exploded that left her feeling responsible. Then while out to supper that evening with her husband, she couldn't stop herself worrying about the dogs at home and whether their barking would disturb the neighbour. This neighbour had screeched at her on the weekend about the dogs. Then during the night a cold broke and she found herself with a temperature and worried intensely about missing work. I interpreted that what she termed 'neurotic' anxiety seemed to be related to incidents involving explosions and anger. I pointed out that she had left the previous session having expressed her pent-up feelings about her mother, and that it had been this that led to feelings of guilt and sadness.

She commented that after the session she had experienced a sensory reaction to her mother – of her smell as a younger figure and that she had cried with relief. But in general she felt like a wreck. 'I was confused and in something of a narcoleptic state. I ground to a halt and took the day off work.' Mrs. D went on to say that she had never been ill and had hardly ever taken time off work. In childhood she was sometimes unwell and could recall the smell of clean linen and the sunlight streaming into the nursery window. She believed she was often downcast as a child when 'the props were taken away'. She mentioned school, and how she dreaded the end of term when a particular hymn was sung in assembly as a prelude to the holidays – she had grown to hate that hymn. There would be no one to play with at home. She had invented imaginary friends. Suddenly, she recalled a term break at university when she had decided to stay on to complete an assignment. The university had become a 'ghost town' and she had felt so lonely and depressed. Mrs. D reflected ruefully that she had obviously been depressed at different times in her past.

I would like to note that when Mrs. D described her depressed mental state as 'impermeable', 'knocked out', 'groggy', 'dead tired', 'shrouded', 'ground to a halt', 'narcoleptic', I took this as evidence of an unconscious identification with a mother with a damaged brain who had progressively slipped away. At the time of her mother's death, no major dysphoric or vegetative symptoms had interfered with her grief. However, now, twenty years later, in a clinical situation she was reliving her experience of loss, but in bringing her mother back to life for that purpose she was also bringing back to life all the hidden suffering associated with that loss. In other words, her original mode of identification (by projection) with her mother had been to foreclose certain aspects of her mourning that at the time were unbearable. This meant that when I spoke to Mrs. D of 'keeping close to her mother', I was referring to her continued use of this narcissistic mode of identification, that I believed was associated with her momentary states of confusion and depersonalization as well as with her vegetative and psychomotor symptoms. On the other hand, her suffering in relation to 'letting go' of her mother was expressed predominantly through mental symptoms, such as withdrawal, apathy, anhedonia, excessive rumination, sadness and longing. Therefore, in addressing a delayed acute mourning of this kind, there is always a 'double depression' to be considered, that is, the suffering derived from holding onto the object in a magical way – in essence a persecutory depression – and the suffering from letting go of the object in guilt – a depressive position depression.

In the case of Mrs. D, interspersed between these different forms of distress were periods of remission from her symptoms that took on a distinctly cyclical pattern. This pattern continued throughout her therapy and manifested itself either in a rapid cycle, such as between sessions, or from one week to the next, or it appeared as a slower cycle occurring at greater intervals. I understood these intervals as reflecting occasions when she was distant from the living and closer to the dead compared to the opposite – being closer to the living and feeling more alive and less 'frozen' herself. What seemed important were the fluctuations in the *quality* of her distress over time and not the elimination of the cycling itself, and in my mind this could be associated with therapeutic improvement.

In Chapter 10, I suggested that the hidden structure of depression is a cyclothymic structure, that is uncovered in the analytic context. By this is not meant a bi-polar structure but a syndrome reflecting a cyclical flow between depressed and manic states that is integral to the morphology of all types of depression. The present case study also reveals this pattern of cycling – but between different subtypes of depression. This is by no means a new idea, certainly not in psychoanalysis, but one that is easily over-looked when nomenclatures are too categorical. I think the current evidence from reviews of the statistics of treatment outcomes unambiguously con-firms this. When 80 per cent of patients with mild depression eventually go on to develop severe depression, does this not suggest that these categorical subtypes are variants of the same condition (Roth and Fonagy 2006)?

The neurotic phase

The presence in Mrs. D of 'neurotic' anxiety, fractiousness, sadness and guilt, in addition to existing vegetative and psychomotor symptoms, seemed to represent a change in the clinical picture that coincided with a lifting into consciousness of negative feelings towards her mother (and father) gleaned from memories of childhood unhappiness. The following three dreams have been chosen to illustrate the conflict of ambivalence within Mrs. D and her attempts to engage with it.

> 1. She was outside a house where there stood an old-fashioned tractor with a cart attached. The cart's progress was delayed because her mother was in

the back under a tarpaulin. She was agitated and incapacitated and Mrs. D needed to calm her. She read her mother a poem about a tiger and this calmed her down. Then she left and awoke feeling sad. Blake's poem *Tyger, Tyger* came to mind in her associations – a beast so strikingly beautiful yet also frightening in its capacity for violence – the complexity of the act of creation.

2. She was wandering in a field among autumn leaves picking up treasures and she found her mother's wedding ring.

3. She was at a public swimming pool up to her chest in the water alongside her mother, who was talking to her. There were swimming lanes and a child was swimming up and down in their lane and had to avoid bumping into them by going round them.

The meaning of these dreams appeared straightforward. They recognized the origin of Mrs. D's present 'neurotic anxiety' in her ambivalence towards her mother and towards the Oedipal couple, that was delaying her forward movement. In recognizing the 'Tyger' in herself she was then able to recover the valued wedding ring, representing the creative couple, as well as to recover in her own mind a more healthy and communicative image of her mother and herself, in which a child part of herself was being more accommodating and considerate.

Mrs. D felt a lot better following these dreams. She had more energy and had recovered 'capacity' – she returned to cooking, but she was not yet able to read. She also found herself nostalgic and thinking of adolescence and she began listening to her favourite piece of music from that time. 'Either a veil has lifted or I'm being manic,' she said. But she found that her response to her husband was still 'dulled', except for a surge of rage towards him when he'd talked over her in the car.

Transference

The next phase, one year into treatment, centred on day-to-day events involving Mrs. D's relationships with family and friends and began to include dreams of the therapist with transference significance. Mrs. D continued to struggle with symptoms – foggy brain, tight chest, exhaustion following sleep – that made her feel increasingly helpless and unsure about the therapeutic process. At these times she considered whether or not to break down all pretences altogether and to allow the wheels to come off – or whether to stop psychotherapy. The clinical picture was indeed very mixed for the next few months with Mrs. D alternating between being 'at death's door' to feeling 'sanguine', but then a pattern emerged in which difficult periods between sessions were followed by relief at the end of the next session. At her work things had taken a notable turn for the better – she reported deriving new pleasure and vitality from 'whipping' through tasks that previously would have sunk her. She also felt more 'motherly' towards her employer.

In one dream Mrs. D was due to attend a session accompanied by her husband and was aware of being very late. For some reason that she could not fathom, my address was in St. Matthews Road and she had not been paying attention and was further delayed, which heightened her anxiety. Her husband, on the other hand, seemed relaxed and she then realized they were actually on their way to another town. In her mind she developed a lie to tell me about her absence — that 'we' had rescheduled the appointment. Her sole association was to St Matthew's Passion — the oratorio depicting the suffering of Christ.

In her next dream the therapist bore a resemblance to a famous author, who told Mrs. D he was a long distance runner. He also told her she was a 'medievalist'. In the dream the feeling was that she wanted the therapist to love her. Her associations were to her wish for her father's love and how 'digging up the past' had revealed how little love she had received from him. Her other association was to the endurance of therapy and that I might become bored with her. I pointed out that the two dreams, taken together, revealed her ambivalence towards psychotherapy and towards me. In the first dream she is shown to join with her husband in triumphing over me by leaving me in the dark as to the truth. Yet her guilty lie then reveals in the second dream how she becomes anxious that, given this treatment with me, I might withdraw my love from her by ceasing to stay the distance. I added that in such a case surely only a Christ-like figure could endure and then forgive such treatment? Mrs. D laughed but then looked downcast. I said she suspected I would be like her father who withdrew his caring if she wasn't cooperative.

Unexpectedly in the next session the focus swung back to her mother. She reported that over the weekend she had descended into a negative spiral of thought about herself. A visitor, in describing a recent incident in her life, had ended off by saying, 'There will be trouble to come.' Mrs. D immediately thought that it would be she who was in trouble. She characterized this feeling as a return to 'neurotic anxiety', in other words, guilt. On the Sunday she reached an absolute low point but by the afternoon there was a change. Her husband had used a turn of phrase that reminded her of her mother, and in her mind's eye her mother stood before her, looking well and contented, and Mrs. D was spontaneously moved to say, 'I'm sorry'.

Summary and discussion

The transference factor of a 'present' figure that could 'endure' Mrs. D's delinquency without retaliation or losing interest in her seemed to fulfil certain intrapsychic conditions that allowed her to apologize to her mother and to free herself somewhat of the trap of guilt. She had identified with such an object and was less disowning of her ambivalence.

The loss of a parent through death, in childhood particularly, but also in adulthood, is easier to bear when a surviving parent is present and available for comfort and reassurance (Furman 1974). The acceptance of loss too is more forthcoming, yet no less painful, when grief can be shared with close family members (Bowlby 1980). Unfortunately, Mrs. D's father approached the death of his wife in a completely different way: he withdrew and hid all his feelings and left her to cope with her own personal mourning as best she could. The key, therefore, in overcoming her depression lay with transforming the image of the father as the aggressor who bore no sympathetic feelings for his wife and daughter and who had apparently denied the family catastrophe.

This proved another painful phase of therapy. As the surviving parent her father was all she had at the time and to some extent she too in facing her own loss buried a significant portion of her feelings in identification with him. How else could the extended delay in her mourning for twenty years be accounted for? In this respect they were 'in it together'.

Hence, at this point in Mrs. D's therapy, there were two factors in her resistance that came to be differentiated. First, while she was open to the pain of bringing her mother back to life in order to complete her mourning, she also persisted in repeating an unconscious union with her mother, as a defence, at the cost of achieving an introjective identification. Like the melancholic she cycled in and out of her symptoms according to which identification was at play, until such time that, in the transference, she was forced to face her ambivalence and accept her guilt. Where somatic symptoms were in the ascendancy, her depression took on a persecutory dimension whether the suffering was located in her head or her body. Where her symptoms were emotional her pain resided in her 'imagination' and involved states of acute solitude and sorrow. However, her secondary resistance centred on her relationship with the father, in which a part of her had identified with him in coping with loss and, like him, had denied certain important feelings. This was acted 'out' during maximal and nominal moments of suffering in her therapy by her not being able to speak of what she was going through to her husband or to her father. It was also acted 'in' by her being unable to express loving and at times erotic feelings towards her therapist.

To accept that she was like her father in this respect proved a difficult pill for Mrs. D to swallow since she had set such a store on him being a bad object, especially in relation to his wife. Any further relief from her depression, however, depended on her courage in resolving her ambivalence in this direction, in other words, in resolving the Oedipal dimension of her depression.

Chapter 12

The depressed child

The scandal of prescribing antidepressants

Children are more resilient than we think. The one thing they try to do when they are sick is to get better.

Anonymous mother

What qualifies for a diagnosis of depression in a child? According to the DSM-IV criteria for children, dysthymic disorder must include depressed mood for one year but no major depressive episode. In addition, two or more of the following must be present with no interval exceeding two months: (1) poor appetite or overeating, (2) insomnia or hypersomnia, (3) low energy or fatigue, (4) low self-esteem, (5) poor concentration or difficulty making decisions, (6) feelings of hopelessness. For major depressive disorder, the criteria are (1) anhedonia, (2) flattened affect or at least three of the following, (3) morning onset of depressed mood not related to loss, (3) premature awakening, (4) mental and physical slowdown or agitation, (5) anorexia or weight loss, (6) acute and inappropriate guilt. It has been pointed out that when a diagnosis is based on symptom count, only implausibly high rates of depressive disorder are produced (Harrington 2002).

How many children who seem unhappy carry symptoms of this nature? Weight or sleep disturbance coupled with a sense of dejection and anhedonia is rare in children but weeping, irritability, headaches, stomach aches, accidents, flashes of aggression and deterioration in school work are more common indicators of depressed mood. This is because children generally express their feelings indirectly, not verbally, and they often communicate their moods in physical ways. While some children show apathy and sadness others become hyperactive or hostile. The *Psychodynamic Diagnostic Manual* (PDM Task Force 2006) asserts that childhood disorders have distinct patterns and should never be considered a precursor to an adult disorder by the same name.

It was Winnicott (1988, p. 87) who pointed out that in the total life of the child, swings appear between times of liveliness punctuated by times of acute misery. This, he said, was a continuation of the emotional lability found in infants and small children. He suggested that, in health, depression is a sign of taking life seriously and a sign of being put in a state of doubt. When children *are* depressed, except for severely deprived children, they rarely present with depressed mood – they present with 'anxious restlessness' and irritability or they try to walk on the roof or run away from home. In this way, suggests Winnicott, a child is organizing a defence against what might be an underlying depression – but it might be something else. Winnicott was the first child psychiatrist to question whether a medical diagnosis is suitable for childhood depression, that is, whether a categorical diagnosis of depression allows any differentiation from the ordinary unhappiness of everyday childhood.

More recently Timimi (2004, 2007) makes a similar point about the medicalization of unhappiness in children but tries to explain how this has come about. He argues that before the 1980s diagnosing a child with depression was infrequent and certainly not treatable with antidepressants. Since then childhood depression has become commonplace owing to what he believes is society's changing view of childhood and its problems. The statistics are certainly frightening – in the United Kingdom alone, since 2003, over 50,000 children were diagnosed with depression and over 170,000 prescriptions a year for antidepressants were issued to people under 18 years old. Moreover, 90 per cent of UK child and adolescent psychiatrists prescribe antidepressants to children (Phillips et al. 2003) and the prescription of antidepressants represents over 30 per cent of *all* their prescribing for *any* childhood disorder (Clark 2004).

Timimi (2007) suggests that one cause of this epidemic of prescribing in the UK can be located in changing socioeconomic circumstances and a prosperous postwar economy that allowed children to become pleasure-seeking consumers, like their parents. This seamless commercialization of children into consumers has been the driving force, he believes, in the use of medicalized terminology to categorize children's feelings of happiness and unhappiness – the pre-eminent model being an adult model.

This brings us to the nub of this chapter. In turning children into miniature adults for consumer purposes, the differences between the adult brain and the child brain are collapsed when it comes to evaluating emotional states. The pubertal brain too, which directs endocrinal changes in the body that are part of normal development, is not the adult brain.[1] These differences are all too easily overlooked when it comes to considering children's psychological problems such as depression, which has long been recognized as having multifactorial aetiology and a different symptom cluster compared to adult-like versions of the disorder. Moreover, on the question of reliability alone, psychiatric comorbidity in childhood depression is so extensive that a diagnosis becomes a lottery in the sense that nearly every child can be diagnosed with at least one other psychiatric condition (Harrington 2002; Rutter and Taylor 2002). These problems, including the overlap in children of symptoms of both mild and chronic depression cast serious doubt upon whether major depressive disorder or dysthymic disorder as clinical categories are useful or appropriate for children.

Furthermore, vast numbers of clinical trials for depressed children have utilized DSM-IV criteria for selecting subjects as well as for rating and measuring changes during and following treatment. Furthermore, low reliability of standardized interviews with children persists notwithstanding the introduction of drawings and puppets when using these measures. Why would researchers be so keen on adapting an adult diagnosis to fit children? What would there be to gain? Surely the only rational justification would be if a major new discovery had been made in a field of depression.

However, the real scandal arises when we examine how a categorical diagnosis determines treatment modality – especially the use of antidepressants for children and adolescents, based on effectiveness for adults. Since 1995 hundreds of clinical trials have been carried out on older children and adolescents to endorse or substantiate the effectiveness of antidepressants – formatively in the prescribing of the tricyclics and currently with the selective serotonin reuptake inhibitors (SSRIs). Drug companies initially led the way with academic and social research playing catch-up when multiple concerns were raised about safety. The elemental question of whether antidepressants were safe or even appropriate for children, notwithstanding the inconclusiveness of early studies (see below), became a mere footnote to the headlong rush to the 'market'. But, to repeat, the Achilles heel of this mountain of research rests on one small but commonsense proposition – that if we accept that childhood depression in its aetiology, clinical picture and course does not mimic adult depression, how relevant scientifically can these studies be? What population are they purporting to make efficacy statements about, and treatment recommendations for?

This chapter is written as a polemic in which I would like to examine the research findings on the efficacy of antidepressants for juvenile depression. This will be a prelude to evaluating the reasons why the practice of prescribing antidepressants for children is so pervasive and universal (Phillips et al. 2003). Furthermore, questions need to be asked about the rational or irrational basis for these practices. It will also be worthwhile examining the arguments made by clinicians in defence of these practices, notwithstanding strong warnings from safety bodies – are these arguments based in science or in magic?[2] The blatant obfuscation and scare tactics used by some researchers and clinicians to justify the use of SSRIs only adds greater weight to the perception that paediatric and psychiatric clinicians are in a terrible and dangerous muddle about diagnosing depression in children. More alarmingly, when moving from diagnosis to treatment with SSRIs, the evidence suggests that clinicians have chosen magic over science.

Since 2002 the BBC *Panorama* programme has been on the trail of the controversy surrounding the prescribing of SSRIs for children (including adolescents). Its first exposé focused on the SSRI Paroxetine (Seroxat in the UK, Aropax elsewhere). Hailed by GlaxoSmithKline (GSK) as a wonder drug at the time, Paroxetine was used to treat major depression, obsessive-compulsive, panic and social anxiety disorders in adult outpatients. But when trials were begun with children and teenagers, it was clear that a new market was being sought for the drug. By gaining access to the company's paediatric clinical trials that had been presented in a lawsuit against the company, it became apparent that Paroxetine increased the risk of suicide in young people rather than reducing it, as the company had claimed in its trials. Worst of all, an internal document came to light that advised staff to withhold clinical evidence from two trials that Paroxetine had little beneficial effect for adolescents. While disclosure of these trails was deemed 'commercially unacceptable' GSK had no reason to panic – by 2003 the sales of Paroxetine had amounted to $4.97 billion worldwide.

The scandal of SSRIs

In its most recent update, *Panorama*'s investigators (2007) hit the jackpot when a box of files belonging to GSK was discovered in an apartment in Malibu, California. They now had greater access to the clinical trials involving hundreds of children and adolescents recruited from around the world who had taken part in the trials for Paroxetine (Seroxat/Aropax). The documents confirmed what had been previously revealed: that Seroxat had not worked for teenagers, that there were side-effects, and that in one clinical trial adolescents were six times more likely to become suicidal after taking it.[3] This meant that the number of suicides or suicide gestures linked to Paroxetine had been significantly underreported to the regulator. The programme tracked down one of the lead scientists, Professor Keller, of Brown University, head of the GSK study, about the failure to highlight suicide risk. He replied, 'None of these suicide attempts led to suicide and very few of them led to hospitalization. The thing is, you have to consider what are the alternatives, right?' It is noteworthy that in five years since the scandal broke no charges were brought by the UK Medicines and Healthcare Products Regulatory Agency against GSK, apparently because of gaps in the legislation on drug safety. Having not licensed Paroxetine for children there was no obligation by GSK to disclose its data about its trials in under-18s!

'You have to consider what are the alternatives, right?'

It was the concern about a suicidal response to Paroxetine that galvanized the medical community, the public and the TV networks. In the UK the BBC received close to 1,400 emails and 5,000 telephone calls – mostly from people who had suffered side-effects and drug withdrawal symptoms. Seven years on, what is the verdict about the safety of antidepressants for children and adolescents – and do they work? In the United States the Treatment for Adolescents with Depression Study (TADS) series, which began in the late 1990s, continues to release results about the efficacy and safety of Prozac in the treatment of young people. These were multiple trials, at several sites, involving large samples, in which combinations of treatment are compared for remission rates. I shall briefly highlight three studies.

Results from one study were released in 2004 on comparing the rates of physical, psychiatric, and suicide-related events in adolescents with major depressive disorder. Subjects were treated for three months by Prozac alone, cognitive-behavioural therapy (CBT), combination treatment, or placebo. Results: depressed adolescents reported high rates of physical symptoms at the start of the study that improved as depression improved. Although twenty-four suicide-related events occurred during the twelve-week period, there were no suicide 'completions'! Psychiatric 'adverse events' and suicide-related events were more common in adolescents treated with Prozac but combination treatment offered a more favourable 'safety profile' than medication alone.

In data published in 2006, 439 adolescents with major depressive disorder were offered a twelve-week treatment programme of Prozac, CBT, their combination, or a placebo. The conclusion was that combination treatment of Prozac and CBT was superior to both monotherapy and placebo, but overall rates of remission remained low and residual symptoms were common at the end of twelve weeks of treatment. In fact, after twelve weeks of treatment only 102 (23 per cent) of 439 youths had achieved the criteria for remission.[4]

In 2008 another set of results were released from the TADS study that focused on long-term effectiveness and safety outcomes. The study compared the effectiveness of Prozac, CBT, and their combination in 327 12–17-year-old adolescents with major depressive disorder (DSM-IV criteria) over a twenty-six-week treatment programme. The Children's Depression Rating Scale (Revised) was used to measure improvement. Findings were that for adolescents with moderate to severe depression, treatment with Prozac alone or in combination with CBT 'accelerated the response'. Adding CBT to medication enhanced the safety of medication. Taking benefits and harms into account, the authors concluded that combined treatment appeared superior to either monotherapy for major depression in adolescents.[5]

Initially, the findings of the 2004 study caused quite a splash, as highlighted by Lenzer (2004), 'Talk and pills best for depression in kids' (CNN.com); 'Prescribed drugs with therapy aid teen depression' (*Wall Street Journal*); 'Combination aids depressed youths' (*New York Times*). The drug companies must have breathed a collective sigh of relief. Their SSRIs had been saved by 'combination therapy' – a gift to the marketers of SSRIs too, who could now reassure the public about safety. Unfortunately, there were some problems with the design of this study (Jureidini et al. 2004a). They claimed that despite their conclusions, Prozac had no statistical advantage over placebo and became so only when added to CBT in an unblinded arm of the study. In addition, other design flaws meant that the claims and conclusions mentioned in the abstract, particularly about reducing suicidality, were not representative of data found in the body of the report – but the American Academy of Child and Adolescent Psychiatry refused to publish his objections. Notoriously, the TADS were ostensibly funded by a government agency but the researchers received funding from the drug industry (Timimi 2007).

But what about the TADS results that show that SSRIs as a monotherapy came off second best for effectiveness in all three studies? And what is to be deduced from the correlation made between efficacy and safety – that CBT 'enhances the safety' of medication and provides a favourable 'safety profile'? This linkage, inadvertently or not, implies that there was clear benefit attributable to Prozac – which was certainly not proved in these trials and is therefore tantamount to an endorsement of SSRIs. Through sleight of hand, therefore, the safety issue concerning medication slips through the net and with the addition of 'therapy', an alibi is created to allow the practice of prescribing SSRIs for children and adolescents to continue unchecked. It is this type of disingenuous 'slip' that has made SSRI research so maddening to digest and which leaves the distinct impression that science is not being well served.

CBT and IPT (interpersonal therapy) are often advanced as the only psychosocial treatments to have been shown efficacy in controlled research. The absence of other therapies in RCT-driven research has been lacking leaving the field clear for these short-term treatments.[6] However, Roth and Fonagy (2006) noted that there were marked differences in results when trials were administered by proponents of CBT compared to other investigators, who in fact found greater rates of relapse in their trials. Nonetheless, there are many studies that have demonstrated clear benefit of CBT for juvenile depression, such as the one by Harrington et al. (1998). On the other hand, with the pace of new research the effectiveness of the role of CBT as an effective partner to SSRI treatment of children has been challenged by Goodyer et al. (2007). In a study of 208 youngsters aged 11–17 the authors found no evidence that combination therapy of CBT plus an SSRI in the presence of routine clinical care or SSRI alone led to improved outcome by twenty-eight weeks. The comparison was with the provision of routine clinical care plus an SSRI alone. On this occasion medication had a better outcome, though in a longitudinal analysis there was no difference in effectiveness of treatment for the primary or secondary outcome measures.

Then in 2008, based on an earlier review of published versus unpublished data (Whittington et al. 2004) the UK Department of Health ended the partnership by endorsing the National Institute for Health and Clinical

Excellence (NICE) guidelines recommending that for depressed children psychological treatments should be offered as an alternative to pharmacology. Furthermore, accompanying this development Alan Johnson, the then UK Health Secretary, in a £170 million scheme, announced that 3,600 new therapists, including 200 child therapists per year, would be trained to provide 'talking treatments' for depression. These new steps took an axe to the root of the incontrovertible view that 'combination therapy' was the best and the safest first-line treatment for depressed youngsters.

Risk–benefit analysis: pragmatism or irrationality?

A risk–benefit analysis refers to a calculation of expected costs weighed against the expected benefits of one or more actions in order to choose the best or the most profitable option. The concept derives from a business model and is sometimes referred to as a 'trade-off'. In drug research a cost–benefit analysis consists of a medical opinion that in prescribing a drug with unknown dangers or side-effects it is better to prescribe than not to prescribe where the alleviation of symptoms is likely or when an illness is life-threatening. Is juvenile depression a life-threatening illness? And if there are known risks and known side-effects for any one treatment, why not try another?

However, there are more convincing grounds on which to challenge the appropriateness and prudence of employing a risk–benefit assessment in the case of juvenile depression. Take the example of tricyclic antidepressant treatment of children. In a systematic review by Hazell et al. (2002) the authors concluded that tricyclics were no more effective than placebo in the treatment of depression in children and adolescents. These drugs had been used for over fifteen years on children and in this review it was made clear that tricyclics were significantly associated with clinically adverse effects (like sudden cardiac arrest) and that they were toxic in overdose. However, before this review the use of tricyclics was pervasive in child psychiatry and had been approved on the balancing of risks and benefits. Clearly such a balancing has nothing to do with science, safety or even pragmatism.

It then becomes a matter of considerable irony, and of great alarm, that the popularization of the SSRIs as first-line medications for depressed children has been rationalized and justified on the basis that they have fewer side-effects that the tricyclics (Kutcher 1997).

According to this logic one can claim that something that is toxic is good on the grounds that it is the better tolerated than something that has been found to be more toxic. Is this science or magic? What it is, plainly, is a distortion of risk–benefit theory and to put such a statement to the test we need consult no further than the ordinary parent who would have little difficulty in recognizing the naivety of this style of logic – as in, 'But Mom! It's OK to have Fanta rather than Coke before bedtime because Fanta's got 2 per cent less sugar.'

Unfortunately, it is precisely this type of logic that permeates the risk–benefit appraisal used by many paediatric clinicians in their prescribing of antidepressant medications for children. One must bear in mind that practically all medications used for children are first tested on adults because of the consent difficulties in conducting studies on children. Therefore, an assumption is made that benefit found for adults logically confers benefit on children, in which case the risk–benefit appraisal goes something like this – when a child is depressed it is better to prescribe something shown to have tested benefit for adults than to do nothing, since if theoretically there is some perceived benefit in symptom alleviation there is less risk of a life-threatening outcome. It is difficult not to perceive this type of appraisal as a justification for conducting unnecessary toxic experiments on children under the guise of medical treatment. A case in point is the 2008 approval by the FDA of the use of Lepraxo, a SSRI previously sanctioned for major depression in adults, for young people aged 12–17. The only other SSRI to be approved for this age group was Prozac. On the basis of only two trials where maintenance efficacy could not be tested, the FDA concluded that maintenance could be 'extrapolated' from the adult data.

Of course, to reinforce this logic the risk that is most drummed up by marketers of antidepressants is the risk of self-injury or suicide during a depressive episode. However, suicide in children is extremely rare – 1.3 per 100,000 in children between the ages of 10 and 14, rising to 8.2 per 100,000 in teenagers aged between 15 and 19, according to the US National Institute of Mental Health.[7] There are no statistics for children under the age of 10. Ironically, and in some cases tragically, Paroxetine was found to increase the risk of suicidal thinking in juvenile depression rather than reducing it, as had been anticipated from adult cases.

Yet the *possibility* of a suicide attempt in depressed youngsters has become a powerful propaganda tool for the advocacy of antidepressant medication. Here are the same statistics mentioned above interpreted on a website, HealthyPlace.com,[8] on a page titled 'Depression in Children', subsection 'The risk of suicide in children'. This site was launched in March 2000 and the website authors claim that in little more than a year, solely by word of mouth, this became the largest consumer mental health site on the internet.

If a child has major depressive disorder, he or she is seven times more likely to try suicide. About 22% of depressed children will try suicide. Looking at it another way, children and teenagers who attempt suicide are eight times more likely to have a mood disorder, three times more likely to have an anxiety disorder, and six times more likely to have a substance abuse problem. A family history of suicidal behavior and guns that are available also increase the risk. The vast majority (almost 90%) of children and adolescents who attempt suicide have psychiatric disorders. Over 75% have had some psychiatric contact in the last year. If a number of these are present, suicide risk needs to be carefully assessed regularly. If children are constantly dwelling on death and think being dead would be kind of nice, they are more likely to make a serious attempt.

The phrase 'kind of nice' relaxes the reader by evoking a folksy, home-on-the-range, 'we are all in it together' type of approach to the subject of depression-related suicide, but the presentation of the statistics is over-wrought and disingenuous in some respects, and the seriousness of child suicide is simply exploited as a scare tactic. Notice how easily the website shifts from 'children' to 'adolescents' in making claims about causes and dangers. Note too the suggestion that depression and suicide are not just statistically but logically linked. As I have mentioned, the incidence of suicide or suicide attempts among pre-pubertal children is rare and very few of these children are ever diagnosed with MDD, hence 'Eight times more likely' must be a tiny minority, but lumping this together with adolescents diagnosed with MDD produces the alarming statistic of 90 per cent. What is the point of stirring up alarm?

The answer lies in the next section on 'Treating Depressed Children'. Here it is stated that generally in mild to moderate depression, psycho-therapy should be tried first, but if there is no response then an antidepressant should be added. What constitutes a response is not defined. In cases of severe depression medication should be recommended at the start of treatment, and the recommended first-line medications for depressed children and adolescents today are the SSRIs. This is due to better tolerance and fewer side-effects than the tricyclics.

Necessity knows no reason, it seems. Unfortunately, the coercive logic of prescription as depicted on the HealthyPlace.com website has become a common feature of the psychiatric intervention in child depression. Putting it all together, the logic of the website advocates that an untreated depression in a child (or adolescent) statistically carries the risk of suicide, and that therefore the risk of not treating must be measured against the risks of using medications whose safety and efficacy have been established only in adults, but not yet in children. This kind of reasoning mimics the logic of the delinquent – an expert in arguing that because something cannot be dis-proved, it must be true, or it must be assumed 'in the mean time' to be true. This is also the logic of oversell, hence it should be no surprise that the sponsors of the HealthyPlace.com website are AstraZeneca Pharmaceuticals, Eli Lilly (Cymbalta), Forest Labs (Lexapro), Pfizer Labs, Glaxo-SmithKline and Wyeth Pharmaceuticals (Effexor).

To round out the present argument: in assessing the advantage and safety of SSRIs (or any drug for children) clearly the issue is not whether some children are better at tolerating potential toxicities, but whether or not children should be exposed *at all* to a class of drugs that in over 50 per cent of studies has never statistically out-performed placebo – while accelerating the risk of adverse actions two- to threefold relative to placebo (Ryan 2005). That is the central scientific issue – statistical advantage. Yet it is extraordinary how often in clinical trials as well as in recommended treatment pathways, it is assumed that SSRIs have already been shown to have clinical advantage over placebo (see below). The one exception has been Prozac. In their study Whittington et al. (2004) conducted a risk and benefits meta-analysis of data from RCT studies that evaluated an SSRI versus placebo in the 5–18 years group and found that while published data suggested a favourable risk–benefit profile for SSRIs, the addition of unpublished data clearly indicated that, except for Prozac, risks would outweigh benefits in the treatment of juvenile depression with these medicines.

The blatant denial and obfuscation that was so evident in the use of tricyclics has been repeated with SSRIs, but on a grander scale. As mentioned above, according to Phillips et al. (2003) 90 per cent of UK child and adolescent psychiatrists prescribe antidepressants to children, while antidepressants represent over 30 per cent of *all* prescribing for *any* childhood disorder (Clark 2004).

But SSRIs work!

Here is a basket of responses made by doctors reacting to critical reviews in the *British Medical Journal* questioning claims of therapeutic benefit of SSRIs in children.

[Criticisms of SSRIs] fly in the face of years of clinical experience with tens of thousands of children and adolescents with major depression in many countries around the world. To deny children treatment for a condition that has a potentially fatal outcome based on studies with flawed design is outrageous and irresponsible.

The conclusion in this case must be that the evidence of benefit does not exist, not that lack of benefit exists. It is important that we do not needlessly dismiss potentially useful drugs when viable alternatives are thin on the ground.

When faced with a 14 year old sexually active depressed child living with a druggie mom and her fifth 'boyfriend' about all I can do as a doctor is refer for counselling, put her on Depo Provera, and give her Prozac. After all, I can only use the tools available to me. Depression is probably biochemical, but don't forget that the 'alternative' to Prozac is alcohol, marijuana, crack, or illicit drugs.

Why such a defensive reaction to evidence of equivocal benefit for SSRIs? If looked at from the point of view of science alone these responses, in subtle and obvious ways, are irrational. The first is a gamble that disavows the requirement of proof over anecdotal opinion. The second gyrates and is similarly not reliant of proof but on anecdotal magic – there is no evidence of benefit but nonetheless benefit exists. And the third, while based on genuine emotion and pragmatism, nonetheless echoes the scaremongering of Professor Keller: 'You have to consider what are the alternatives, right?' No one can deny the formidable responsibilities that child mental health specialists face in managing depression through antidepressants, especially GPs, who are often not in a position to offer therapy other than drug therapy. But in questioning this treatment path, Timimi (2007) points out:

> Given the high placebo response, many doctors will see improvements after prescribing an antidepressant for a young person in distress and subsequently attribute improvements to the drug. This high placebo response may thus reinforce prescribing, and it has been difficult for many doctors faced with a distressed young person to accept that SSRIs may be ineffective.
>
> (Timimi 2007, p. 751)

Yet it is nonetheless true that anecdotal reports by teachers, parents and child therapists of improvements in children on SSRIs are common. Is this a therapeutic effect, or a placebo effect or a random effect quite unrelated to pharmacology? Whittington et al. (2004) were surprised that different SSRIs that share the same pharmacodynamic mechanism presented different benefit–risk ratios in childhood depression, especially as these ratios are generally regarded as clinically equivalent in adults. This finding suggests that antidepressants work in some children but not in others, which of course gives rise to unreliable results. Or else, it means that SSRIs are simply a chemical treatment that has a scattershot effect – similar to the tricyclics. In this study the authors add, pressingly, that the non-responders remain at full risk of an adverse drug reaction.

In their defence paediatric clinicians have attempted to justify their continued reliance of SSRIs in two ways. When in early 2000 the controversy broke about the possibility that Paroxetine might induce suicidality in some patients, there was a pause for breath. In print, a new (to me) phrase was born – 'clinical equipoise', as in the statement, 'a position of clinical equipoise should be adopted on this issue'. In other words, do nothing now while further clarification takes place on the matter. Other phrases such as 'warnings and monitoring are more likely to reduce overall risks' and 'optimal suicide reduction strategy should be put in place' (Healy and Whitaker 2003) all suggest a kind of equivocating and moral failure in taking responsibility for a major clinical crisis.

Another justification came in the form of pointing out the poverty of research on alternatives. The alternative of child psychotherapy has often been singled out for two reasons, first, that randomized controlled trials (RCTs) have not yet been routinely undertaken, or where they have been undertaken they have not proven effectiveness, and second, that child psychotherapy is time consuming and therefore not cost-effective. At this point the sophistry and hypocrisy of such views demands that we withdraw our sympathy – especially from child psychiatrists – regarding their difficulties in working their way around cautionary notices and juggling with treatment choices. If they insist on due scientific process of RCTs, peer review, publication and duplication to demonstrate benefit for psychotherapy why are they content to 'carry on prescribing' without the same criteria being fully met for antidepressant medication?

The thorny truth is that since 2000 favourable anecdotal reports have not been substantiated by convincing clinical evidence and that in spite of clear warnings from control bodies, a high proportion of depressed children and adolescents are still likely to be prescribed SSRIs, notably Prozac, Cypramil and Zoloft for no other rational reason that such a practice has reached a critical mass that is too onerous to adjust or reverse. This indicates the scale of the moral failure in the mental health community concerning these medications and it reflects the degree to which both child psychiatry and the general public have been drawn into a collective fantasy that for children SSRIs have a proven track record.

It is noteworthy that when the cracks were exposed in this track record, a new clinical mantra was forthcoming – 'in mild to moderate depression psychotherapy should be tried first, followed by an SSRI should there be no response'. For children this is simply fudging of the issue of safety and benefit. How many child psychiatrists (or GPs) in private practice refer children for psychotherapy as a first-line treatment for diagnosed depression? Michels (2000) diagnoses the problem as a professional one. Armed as they are nowadays with state-of-the-art medications, child psychiatrists have raised their status among their medical colleagues who for years frowned upon their quasi-psychologically based diagnoses and treatments. Now they can boast evidenced-based justification and support for a purely biomedical approach towards treating depression, especially evidence from research on new medications.

For young patients and their parents these developments should be a cause for alarm rather than celebration. Consider the situation of a teenager unlucky enough to receive a diagnosis of bi-polar disorder where it has become axiomatic that an additional mood stabilizer be prescribed should that person have an adverse reaction to an SSRI!

Chapter 13

Freud's depression

Between 1923, when it was first diagnosed, and the time of his death, Freud underwent a succession of surgical procedures for cancer of the mouth – in total thirty-three operations over a sixteen-year period. He had been a heavy smoker – twenty cigars a day since the age of 24 – but he regarded smoking as a necessary accompaniment to his productivity as well as one of the greatest and cheapest enjoyments in life. When he tried to stop, he developed tachycardia, arrhythmia, hypomania (including visions), depression and a dread of dying. When digitalis controlled the racing of his heart, his depression got worse. Freud commented, 'It is annoying for a doctor who has to be concerned all day long with neurosis not to know whether he is suffering from a justifiable or hypochondriacal depression' (Jones 1953, I, p. 340). After fourteen months Freud resumed smoking. In assessing his nicotine addiction, he reassured himself that his father, a heavy smoker too, had lived to the ripe old age of 81. No interpretation of a neurotic basis of smoking relating to his father is forthcoming from biographers like Jones, though his depression about giving up has been ascribed to his rather adolescent battle with Fliess – a friend and father figure – over the dangers of smoking (Schur 1972, p. 42).

All in all, Freud had five prostheses fitted for his cancerous upper jaw. They had to be inserted in the morning and removed in the evening, causing him ongoing pain when speaking and eating. He referred to the cancer as his 'dear old carcinoma' and when once informing Marie Bonaparte of the latest treatment he wrote, '[T]he radium has once again begun to eat away at something . . . and my world is what it was previously, a small island of pain floating on an ocean of indifference.'

Psychologically, Freud's personal physician Max Schur (1972, p. 60) believed Freud suffered less from anxiety than from excessive mood swings 'which at their low ebb had a definite depressive quality.' He also described Freud's tendency to obsessively brood about death and his dying at a designated age of 51 – a legacy of his close relationship with Fliess, who developed an idiosyncratic theory of bio-numerological periods that predicted events like death.

In describing the intervals in Freud's life where he suffered from depression, material from his biographies as well as correspondence with and between colleagues and family will be widely drawn upon to illustrate the various contexts and events during which these bouts of depression occurred. Many of these biographical items have been previously reported in countless books and journal articles but to my knowledge, none have chosen the specific focus of depression. My goal is to show how painful childhood experiences involving loss and guilt formed a pathway in Freud for depression, beginning in early adult life with the death of his father. It was this depression that spurred him on to carry out a systematic self-analysis that guided both his intellectual understanding of depression as well as fuelling the discovery of many essential concepts that, in time, became the bedrock of psychoanalysis. In common with the other authors that appear below, Klein and Bion, traumatic life events like death, illness, conflictual relationships, guilt, migration and war, along with acute struggles with the creative impulse, would play a significant role in the aetiology of depression.

Early Freud

Being a much sought-after firstborn, a son, and his mother's favourite – her 'goldener Sigi' – Freud enjoyed all those rights and privileges that would later fuel his intellectualism and his ambition. At the age of 1½, however, a baby brother Julius was born, depriving him of his special status. Freud deeply resented his new brother, as he did his sister Anna, who came next, but Julius died at the age of 6 months from a gastrointestinal problem. In later life Freud told Fliess, 'I greeted my one-year-younger brother . . . with adverse wishes and genuine childhood jealousy; and . . . his death left the germ of [self] reproaches in me' (Freud–Fliess, 3 October 1897, p. 268).

In his painstaking research into Freud's self-analysis, particularly as reflected in his dreams, Anzieu (1986) links Freud's rivalry and death wishes towards other figures in his dreams to the lasting feelings of guilt about his brother Julius. He also refers to Grinstein's (1980) claim that in one dream of 6 December 1898, the dreamer Freud deflected his guilt about Julius onto his mother, suggesting that if only she had taken better care of him, he would have survived.

So it would be the 'germ' of guilt derived from rivalry and ambivalence towards Julius, followed by his sudden disappearance, that would have mobilized some of Freud's later depressive responses to similar life events and situations. Freud himself commented during his self-analysis that it was these malevolent wishes towards Julius and an older nephew John that determined what was neurotic in all his later friendships. The psychology of self-reproach became a subject that Freud explored with great authority throughout his writings with its role in depression arguably receiving a definitive statement in 'Mourning and melancholia' (1917). This statement will enable us to identify the nature or type of depression that Freud himself suffered from.

With regard to depression, there are two other factors in Freud's early life that are also worth considering. First, his mother Amalia, ten years younger than her husband, was almost continuously pregnant until Freud was 10 years old – there would be five more daughters and another son born in that timespan. It therefore seems likely that, in spite of being described as his mother's indisputable golden boy, Freud had to contend with an endless string of replacements and rivals for his mother's love. Second, as a small child Freud had a nurse named Monica, a woman similar in age to his father, to whom he became very attached. At about the same time as Julius died, when he was 1½, she suddenly disappeared. In his forties, Freud learned from his mother that she had been dismissed and jailed for stealing money from the family – in fact, he was told she had stolen some coins and toys from the boy Freud himself, as his mother reported it! I mention these two factors to support the idea of a pathway in Freud, for both guilt-based depression and for depression from acute ambivalence and rivalry, factors that would later provide the two corner-stones of his insights into the psychology of mourning and melancholia. Another factor added by Anzieu (1986) is an identification with a sick or lost object.

The cocaine episode

Freud experimented with cocaine during two periods 1884–1887 (Jones 1953, I, p. 86) and from late 1892 continuing into the middle or late 1890s (Thornton 1984). He was 28 years old, engaged to Martha Bernays and struggling to establish himself as a successful neurologist in Vienna. To his fiance, who lived with her parents in a distant town, he wrote in an obviously thrilled state,

> Woe to you, my Princess, when I come [for a planned visit]. I will kiss you quite red and feed you until you are plump. And if you are forward you shall see who is the stronger, a gentle girl who doesn't eat enough or a big wild man who has cocaine in his body. In my last severe depression I took coca again and a small dose lifted me to heights in a wonderful fashion. I am just now busy collecting the literature for a song of praise to this magical substance.
>
> (quoted in Jones 1953, I, p. 93)

As a young man Freud was known to have suffered from periodic depressions and anxiety attacks that were much in evidence during his long engagement to Martha (Jones 1953, I, p. 93). In cocaine he had undeniably discovered a formidable antidepressant for his depressive responses to her absences. Yet given that he used pure, concentrated cocaine, and used it frequently and often in powerful doses, it is certain that he would have suffered from cocaine withdrawal symptoms, notably depression. This cycle would probably have resulted in an addiction.

Freud's angst at this time was related to establishing a career and overcoming his financial problems. His scientific ambitions were strong but he needed to earn a living as a neurologist, facing stiff obstacles in the overcrowded professional environment of Vienna. He felt like an outsider too, especially when encountering flashes of anti-Semitism. His first successful piece of scientific work, undertaken while still a student, involved dissecting 400 eels to verify the existence of testes! However, his experience with cocaine gave him the idea of promoting this new wonder drug for its antidepressant qualities. He published a monograph on the subject – *Uber Coca* in July 1884 – but unfortunately he failed to capitalize on the drug's anaesthetic properties, leaving the field open to a colleague Karl Koller to whom he had introduced the drug.

In the same year Koller presented a report to the Medical Society (*Billrothhaus*) describing ways in which cocaine could be used as a general anaesthetic for delicate eye surgery. His success was assured when this type of local anaesthetic spread to ophthalmology, dentistry, and other areas of medical practice. In telling the story of how years later Koller diagnosed glaucoma in Freud's father and administered, with Freud's assistance, cocaine as a local anaesthetic before his eye operation, Jones (1953, I, pp. 95–96) seems to underscore Freud's defeat. There is some evidence Freud continued his cocaine use for many years. Thornton (1984) claims that it was Freud's cocaine use that ruined his sex life after the age of 40.

Death of father

In October 1896, when Freud was 40 years old, his father Jacob died at the age of 81 of natural causes. An anguished Freud wrote to Fliess, dubbed by some as his analyst:

> [T]he old man's death affected me deeply . . . I valued him highly . . . with his peculiar mixture of deep wisdom and his fantastic light-heartedness he had a significant effect on my life. By the time he died his life had long been over but in my inner sense the whole past has been reawakened by this event. I now feel quite uprooted.
>
> (Freud–Fliess, 2 November 1896, p. 202).

For 'uprooted' Freud used the German word *entwurzeltes*, meaning naked, exposed, raw.

Freud revered his father but he botched the funeral arrangements by not arranging a ceremony (as his father had in fact wished), which caused the family social embarrassment. Then on the night following the funeral he had a dream (*the Close the Eyes Dream*) which has been interpreted as an infantile wish to kill his father (see Anzieu 1986, p. 172). Some say that psychoanalysis began with this dream, as Freud was so struck by the dream's complex meaning, and its intensely depressing effect, that he immediately put himself into analysis – a self-analysis. The self-analysis became a vehicle for mourning, not only for his father but also for other depressing events from childhood brought to life during this systematic self-enquiry. There were times when his self-analysis generated depression and times when the analysis, and the creative evidence drawn from it, acted as a sublimation of depression. Based on his own feelings Freud would later claim, in the Preface to the Second Edition of *The Interpretation of Dreams* (1900, p. 317), that a father's death is 'the most significant event, the most decisive loss of a man's life'.

Depression in self-work and in publication

Spending hours in extreme boredom, turning from one thing to another, cutting open books, playing patience or chess but not able to persist for long, consciousness inhibited and veiled, emotionally blunted as to work. These are some of the symptoms enumerated by Jones (1953, I, p. 336) to describe Freud's mood during the 1890s when he reached in his own words 'a profound inner crisis'. According to Jones, this was clearly a severe depression and its timing can be linked to the death of his father, his painful withdrawal from his friend and mentor Fliess, and the start of his self-analysis – described by Freud as 'harder than any other'.

Chief among those personal issues absorbing his mind was whether his father had been an abuser or not. Using dreams depicting incestuous longings he was persuaded that this was not the case, but the humbling consequence was that he had give up the keystone of his theory of the causation of neurosis – an unpleasant passive sexual experience in childhood followed by a pleasant active sexual experience. From this troubled period, however, emerged the discovery of the Oedipus complex as well as an astonishing body of work beginning with the publication of *The Interpretation of Dreams* (1900) and *Three Essays on the Theory of Sexuality* (1905).

The publication of his first book, however, resulted only in a fresh bout of depression. With all the painstaking work of personal soul-searching behind him, he experienced the book's completion as an utterly painful anti-climax. He stated that it felt more like letting go of emotional rather than intellectual property. His depression was confounded by the paltry sales figures (only 351 copies in the first six months) and the lukewarm reception in reviews. In reading one 'kind' yet condescending review in a lay journal, he was ready to 'explode with rage' (Newton 1995, p. 222). Instead, he slipped into a vegetative state of irritability and despondency and shelved plans to write another book. In a letter to Fliess he wrote, 'There has never been a six month period in which I so constantly and ardently longed to be living in the same place as you . . . You know that I have been going through a deep inner crisis . . . you would see how it has aged me' (Freud–Fliess, 23 March 1900).

Similarly, Freud suffered what Gay (1995) described as 'postpartum depressions' following the completion of *Totem and Taboo* and *The Ego and the Id*. When struggling with creative work, or when lonely, disillusioned and lacking confidence, Freud often sought comfort and reassurance from friends and colleagues (Schur 1972, p. 222). In this mood he would disparage his work or claim he was ready to throw in the towel. His correspondence is littered with such examples – of exhortations and appeals for solace and sympathy with his struggles over the creative impulse. However, once he unburdened himself he usually bounced back, often spectacularly, which occasionally gave the impression of a neurotic factor of the 'cry wolf' type. But this would be unfair: Reich (1968) once pointed out that pioneers like Freud needed colleagues and co-workers but they were not always available, or were often full of their own demands, and this could lead to hours of loneliness and restless waiting for someone to call. He once observed Freud from the street below, alone, and pacing up and down in his rooms 'like a caged animal'.

The Great War

There is an impressive photograph on display at 19 Bergasse – now the Freud Museum, Vienna – of Freud, aged 58, seated with his two sons Martin and Ernst, both of whom are in uniform. The mood seems relaxed and agreeable, as if they had just shared a joke, and there is an air of virility in their collective postures. Yet the way in which both sons are draped in darkness while their father is fully lit strikes an eerie, even ominous, tone. The year was 1916 and both sons were probably on leave from the Front, where they had already seen action.

Many years earlier, during his medical training, when Freud was about the same age as his sons, he was called up to do a year's military training. Apparently there were few duties and he spent most of his time reading philosophy and translating John Stuart Mill into German. His one highlight was being arrested for being absent without leave (AWOL) on his twenty-fourth birthday! Six years later, now qualified, he was called up again for a month on a training manoeuvre in Moravia. The tedium and phoniness of 'playing at war', as well as his derisory assessment of the senior officers, is captured in a letter to Breuer on 1 September 1886 (Jones 1953, I, p. 211), but Freud obviously toed the line because he mentions in the letter that he has not yet been confined to barracks. His complaints would be echoed by Bion, who also fought in the Great War, on the opposite side, and who also lashed out at the idiocy and mindlessness of war, especially among officers who in casually issuing orders were sending hundreds of soldiers to certain death.

Freud's son Martin joined the artillery and was deployed on the Russian front while Ernst saw action in Galicia. Freud's second son Oliver was recruited as an engineer for the army to build tunnels and barracks. Freud had a dream in which the death of all his sons was depicted. To his surprise he discovered that Martin had been wounded in the arm on the same day as the dream. The dream underscores the fear, helplessness and desolation felt by those with loved ones serving on far-flung borders. Everyone was hoping for a quick victory but the conflict dragged on and on, with Freud becoming more and more appalled by the barbarian methods of conducting the war.

According to Clark (1982, p. 376) Freud entered the year 1915 with a depression. 'At present I am as in a polar night and am waiting for the sun to rise', he confided to Abraham. The flow of patients had dried up and he was forced into utilizing his time giving lectures and writing a series of papers on 'metapsychology'. His mood turned to despair when he heard of the death of his half-brother Emanuel, who on a trip to England, fell off a train and died. In another letter to Abraham, he wrote:

> Life bears heavily on me . . . I believe I have had my time, and I am not more depressed than usual . . . and console myself with the assurance that my work lies in the good hands of men such as you and Ferenczi.
> (Freud–Abraham, 20 May 1977, p. 261)

After four gruesome years the Armistice ultimately arrived on 11 November 1918. This brought considerable relief, but his son Martin had not yet contacted Freud. In December letters arrived in which Freud learned that Martin was alive as a prisoner of war in Italy. Another long year had to be endured before he was released. However, while his sons survived, the Freud family would nonetheless suffer a significant and unexpected loss in the wake of the war.

Freud harboured a longstanding fear of personal death and doubtless during these harrowing years similar acute fears arose concerning the safely of his children. While at the start of the war he and his Austro-Hungarian colleagues were quite gung-ho about their prospects, it must have soon become apparent that the chances of those seeing action surviving the war were extremely low. In the end an astonishing 800,000 Austro-Hungarian soldiers perished, so it was remarkable that only one member of Freud's family – his sister Rosa's son – was cut down in Italy.[1]

Freud experienced the war as wholly destructive, as stripping away the pretensions of civilized humans and exposing the illusion of humanity as authentically and fundamentally good. 'When I speak of disillusionment, everyone will know at once what I mean,' Freud (1915a) said in summarizing its most pervasive effect. He took the view that such a global war, where over 15 million people were slaughtered, had exposed human obsession and pleasure for destruction and deeply questioned human frailty and fitness for civilization. In one of his metapsychology papers, he developed the idea of a death drive, an undoing force in the personality that could be acted out in destructiveness or self-destructiveness, especially in opposing help in overcoming personal problems (Freud 1920).

Death of Sophie and her son 'Heinerle'

Sophie was the fifth arrival in the Freud household and was known as Freud's 'Sunday's child' named after the niece of Freud's Hebrew teacher. She was a homely child and teenager and moved out only with the announcement of her engagement in 1912. She married Max Halberstadt the following year, a photographer from Hamburg, who took several photographs of Freud, including the famous sepia photograph of a stony-faced Freud holding a cigar.

Their first son Ernst Wolfgang was born on 11 March 1914. 'Little Ernst', as he was known, was the inspiration for Freud's 'da–fort' conception of symbolic play based on his observation of the little boy's use of a cotton reel as a vehicle for managing his mother's comings and goings (Freud 1920). Ernst's development was supervised by Hug-Hellmuth, one of the earliest exponents of psychoanalytic work with children. Four years later another son, Heinz Rudolf, called 'Heinerle', was born in Schwerin, a city in northern Germany.

Sophie Halberstadt-Freud died on 25 January 1920, a victim of the Spanish flu pandemic that swept across post-war Europe. Two days later Freud wrote to Pastor Pfister:

> This afternoon we received the news that our sweet Sophie in Hamburg had been snatched away by influenzal pneumonia, snatched away in the midst of glowing health, from a full and active life as a competent mother and loving wife, all in four or five days, as though she had never existed . . . Tomorrow she is to be cremated, our poor Sunday child!
>
> (Freud–Pfister, 20 January 1920, pp. 77–78)

Freud's phrase 'in the midst of glowing health' must have referred to the fact that Sophie had been pregnant with her third child.

Following Sophie's death the younger of her sons, Heinerle, was taken in by Freud's eldest daughter, Mathilde, who was childless. In spite of being a sickly child, he was adored by everyone. Freud called him 'an enchanting fellow . . . I myself know that I have hardly ever loved a human being, certainly never a child, so much as him' (Freud–Kata and Lajos Levy, 11 June 1923). When the boy was diagnosed with miliary tuberculosis, however, it became clear that his end was near. The boy went into a coma, occasionally waking up and chatting normally. Freud commented, 'After each waking and going to sleep one loses him all over again. I don't think I have ever experienced such grief; perhaps my own sickness contributes to the shock.' A very touching and rarely seen photograph of Freud with his grandsons Ernst and a poorly looking Heinerle is on view at the Freud Museum in Vienna. Heinerle died in June 1923, three years after his mother's death, aged 4½.

Freud was heartbroken again. Jones (1957, III, p. 96) comments that this was the only occasion in his life that Freud was known to shed tears. In his own words Freud wrote, 'Fundamentally, everything has lost its meaning for me.' 'I am taking this loss so badly, I believe that I have never experienced anything harder'. When three years later Ludwig Binswanger lost a son, Freud explained, 'For me, that child took the place of all my children and other grandchildren, and since then, since [his] death, I have no longer cared for my grandchildren, but find no enjoyment in life either' (Freud–Binswanger, 15 October 1926). Clearly the death of both Sophie and Heinerle in such close proximity turned normal grief into despair. The hope and promise that little Heinerle might have provided a consolation, even a replacement, for Sophie's loss had been snatched away.

In the following month, when replying to Ferenczi for forgetting his birthday, Freud clarified that no slight was intended, 'Rather, it is connected with my present distaste for life. I have never had a depression before, but this now must be one' (Freud–Ferenczi, 18 July 1923). Four years later, in 1928, he confided in Ernest Jones, 'Sophie was a dear daughter, to be sure, but not a child. It was only three years later, in June 1923, when little Heinerle died, that I became tired of life permanently'.[2]

As Freud mentions, his depression at this juncture was also tied to the state of his own health. Four months before Heinerle's death, at the age of 67, he was diagnosed with cancer of the mouth. While he denied a malignancy – he chose a rhinologist over a cancer specialist to treat him – he must have seen the alarm on the faces of those around him (Gay 1995, p. 419). In the next five years Freud underwent two radical surgeries and other minor operations together with the insertion of many prostheses to his upper jaw, all of which must have taken their toll on his mental state.

The loss of Sophie and Heinerle in conjunction with the news of cancer diagnosis would have deepened Freud's characteristic pessimism about the future. His physician Schur (1972, p. 361) confirmed this by commenting that, psychologically, Freud's grief over Heinerle and his reaction to his cancer diagnosis merged into one another, causing a fatalistic depression.

The company of wolves

In 1928, the year of Freud's seventy-second birthday, Freud went on holiday accompanied by his first dog – a female chow named Lun Yug. Unfortunately, in little over a year, she ran off one day while on a walk and was found dead on a train line. Jones (1957, III, p. 150) reported that Freud was very distressed, comparing the loss of the dog with the loss of a child, in quality if not in intensity. A new dog was sought and another female chow, named Jo-Fi, became Freud's new companion. Most chows have a lion-like appearance and a regal manner, which is probably why her nickname was 'Golden lioness', which is interesting in the light of Freud's own nickname given to him by his mother – 'goldener Sigi'.

Jo-Fi – meaning 'beautiful' in Hebrew – also became a companion to all of Freud's patients, since her customary place of rest was at the foot of his couch. Freud claimed Jo-Fi could intuit the emotional state of the patient: if she stayed put the patient was calm, but if the patient was tense she moved to another part of the room. The story is also told by Freud's son Martin of how Freud never used his watch to determine the end of the session but relied proudly on Jo-Fi – if she sat up and yawned that meant fifty minutes was up. A rumour circulated among patients that Jo-Fi actually conducted the analysis and wrote up the case reports.

Chows are renowned for their loyalty to one master; in fact, it appears that Jo-Fi was offered to Freud as a compensation for the defection of Otto Rank from the Freudian circle (Burlingham 1989, p. 193). Jo-Fi was therefore quite possessive of Freud and when her sister Lun was introduced into the household, this dog had to be taken in by Dorothy Burlingham. In January 1937 Jo-Fi died after an initially successful operation of ovarian cancer. 'Apart from any mourning, it is very unreal', he wrote to the German novelist Arnold Zweig, 'and one wonders when one will get used to it. But, of course, one cannot easily get over seven years of intimacy.' Freud was so upset that he insisted the boarded chow Lun now be returned to him. As Freud grew older, he reputedly preferred the company of chows to people, finding them less bothersome and without a trace of ambivalence.

In the preceding December Freud himself underwent a gruelling operation for his mouth cancer that left him with 'lock jaw'. He carried on seeing patients, using a hot water bottle to hold against his cheek for comfort. To Marie Bonaparte he wrote:

> I [also] get slight relief from short wave therapy, but it does not last long. I am told I have to put up with this existence for another week. I wish you could have seen what sympathy Jo-Fi shows me in my suffering, just as if she understood everything.
>
> (quoted in Jones 1957, III, p. 224)

Was her own cancer an example of her renowned intuition and empathy with Freud?

By February 1939 Freud's cancer had finally been diagnosed as incurable and inoperable. Jones (1957, III, p. 261) captured the bleakness of the end by describing how when Lun was brought to visit him, she retreated to a corner of the room from the odour of the ulcerated cancer that had broken through his cheek. Freud must have known the end was nigh; his friend and physician Schur set in motion the pledged assisted suicide by administering the necessary morphine. It seems that Lun, like Jo-Fi, 'understood' a great deal about Freud's condition.

Conclusion

If depression is a disease of the ego, then subjectively depression manifests itself differently in different people. The reactions to depression are similarly different. With respect to trauma psychoanalysis has taught us that some people are crippled by a relatively small trauma while others manage their saturation in a profound trauma 'expectedly well'. So too with depression. Some people are defeated by depression while others suffer with it bravely and with fortitude. The more fortunate ones are capable of sublimating aspects of their depression into creative work or into life tasks, such as sporting achievements or bringing up children. Freud was surely a brilliant example of such a person. Schur (1972, p. 71) suggests that Freud's compulsive work was both followed by depression and also served as a flight from depression – a type of self-cure from personal hardship and suffering. Anzieu (1986, p. 577) also claimed that Freud used theory as a defence against depression. Yet what we find is that his most acute depression occurred when dealing with his personal demons – during the 1890s – when he carried out his self-analysis, and that it was this depression that spawned his most revolutionary discoveries – his theory of dreams, of infantile sexuality and of the Oedipus complex. As for Freud's own view – he consistently deplored the idea that his theories originated from personal experience instead of from the keen application of the science of the unconscious.

To conclude, Freud never suffered a depressive breakdown in the sense of total loss of function requiring seclusion or convalescence. Nor did he become disabled by tormenting guilt to the point that his personality became melancholic. As a young man he suffered disabling mood swings during his search for success and during his separations from his future wife-to-be. Then when his father died his mourning took on clinical features. As his experience of personal family loss accumulated, and his cancer became a menacing backdrop to his life, his reactions began to resemble many typical features of depression – starting with a loss of interest in intimacy,[3] feeling distant from others, seeking no new relationships, enjoying less and less of previous activities, getting bored and having to endure life events.

His other significant emotional losses – and they were numerous – occurred within the ranks of the psychoanalytic movement itself. Breuer, Fliess, Abraham, Adler, Stekel, Rank, Jung – all men, and at one time all indisputable colleagues, some indelible counterparts and much loved friends (even during difficult times) were lost either to death or to disagreements over one controversy or another – over scientific diversions or dissensions, soured personal relations or political gerrymandering. The part played by Freud's own blatant but often repressed hostility in these falling-outs should not be ignored – and they were certainly not ignored by him. He owned up on several occasions to his intense conflicts of ambivalence towards those male colleagues that meant the most to him, the principal figure being his close friend Fliess, which he put down to an erotic undercurrent that had to be covered over with aggression.

Chapter 14

Klein's depression

Until Grosskurth's (1986) biography the existence of Melanie Klein's depression was probably a little known public fact. While she refers to depression in her unpublished memoir, she gives little sense of her many relapses. Even within the psychoanalytic community in Britain, where she eventually settled, there would have been but a handful of people with knowledge of it, with only a small proportion of these – perhaps her closest colleagues and supporters – aware of the fact that she had gone into analysis with both Sándor Ferenczi, her first analyst, and later with her second analyst Karl Abraham, for acute depression. Perhaps as she was gaining a foothold in the British Psychoanalytical Society – eventually becoming the first European analyst to become a member – people were more preoccupied with fathoming who she was as a personality, and quite how she had arrived at her revolutionary ideas of working with pre-latency children. Moreover, she presented these ideas with such enthusiasm and vigour that depression would have been a distant thought in people's mind (Segal 1979, p. 173). In time, however, and as her role in the society became more established – and more complex – they may have wondered how she coped with the experience of initial acceptance and high praise – Jones defended her unstintingly to Freud as 'a sane, well-balanced and thoroughly analysed person' – followed by subsequent trenchant and partisan opposition to her ideas and methods, especially when it rang out from her own daughter.

Grosskurth's (1986) achievement has been in bringing to light, with the help of correspondence recovered in 1983, little known details of Klein's childhood, her experience as a young mother, her struggles in her marriage, her disappointments in love and her many losses – all of which can be brought to bear on a discussion about her depression. In addition, there needs to be some analysis of how this depression played a part in her creative output – in her new additions to developmental theory, to psychoanalytic theory generally, as well as to subjects like the therapeutic goals of analysis. I shall therefore be drawing extensively on Grosskurth's work and the correspondence therein to describe the lifecycle contexts that contributed to, and sustained, depression in Klein's life more or less as a continuous factor.

Death and tragedy

Melanie was the fourth and youngest child of the Reizes family. When she was born her eldest sibling Emilie was 6 years old, Emmanuel, her brother, was 5 years old, and her youngest sister Sidonie 4 years old. Her father, a general practitioner, in his second marriage, was 55 years old when she was born. Even though she was the youngest, which made her special, she was not by all accounts her father's favourite. Yet he encouraged her to be like him and study medicine, which fuelled her aspirations – at an early age she planned to specialize in psychiatry (Grosskurth 1986, p. 16). In getting engaged at the age of 18, however, a year after her father's death, she had to surrender her ambitions – a disappointment that became a lifelong regret (Segal 1979).

When Melanie was 4 years old, Sidonie died after what is assumed to be a long illness. Such an illness must have been a constant worry to the family and given that her father was a doctor, it would have absorbed much of the parents' attentions and energies. Sidonie was distinctly aware of her own impending death and spent many hours teaching her little sister how to read and write. She believed she was bequeathing to Melanie all that she knew (Segal 1979, p. 29). In her memoir Klein comments that she never got over the feeling of grief for her sister's death, which was compounded, she felt, by her mother's suffering. Grosskurth (1986, p. 15) adds the bleak but truthful comment that this would be the first of a long series of deaths that interspersed Melanie's life. When her father died, Melanie was 17 years old but, in terms of grief, the fact that there was little evidence to suggest a bereavement (she could not recall his ever having played with her) leads Grosskurth (1986, p. 11) to conclude that Melanie's relationship with her father was without depth.

In contrast Grosskurth devotes an entire chapter to Klein's relationship with her older brother Emmanuel and his eventual tragic fate. She depicts him as the spoilt prince of the family whose sense of entitlement stemmed from a serious childhood illness that cut short his life expectancy. At a tender age, he fell ill with scarlet fever, superseded by rheumatic fever, which left him with a weakened heart. The situation was aggravated when during his convalescence, his mother permitted him to join the family on a trip. He suffered a costly relapse that spelt doom for the future.

Using family letters recovered in 1983, Grosskurth paints a picture of a young man who, faced with an uncertain future, used this as an alibi for vanity, self-destructiveness, and a false sense of his own talents. While he had artistic pretensions – writing, painting and music – he initially enrolled to study medicine as his father had done. However, after a few months

Emmanuel dropped out and transferred to the arts school. Shortly thereafter he decided to leave Vienna. With one child already lost to the family, and another saddled with a poor prognosis, this decision must have been difficult but the family resolved that he should be free to pursue his special interests in the arts – in European countries with the advantage of less inclement weather. The young man subsequently launched himself into a peripatetic lifestyle supported by an allowance from his mother. According to Grosskurth (1986, p. 18) this was a death sentence.

From Emmanuel's letters there can be no doubt of the intense bond between Melanie and her brother. Their mother was both jealous and fearful of its incestuous nature. Grosskurth (1986, p. 31) highlights Emmanuel's insecurity abroad and his prurient interest in other people's lives, especially other women's love lives, including Melanie's relationship with her new fiancé, Arthur. In this he appears to be very much like his intrusive mother Libussa, though his mixed feelings towards her were also very strong, as suggested in how he used his allowance – his lifeblood – for gambling and other excesses. When it comes to dynamics such as these, Grosskurth (1986) falls short of understanding the complexities that would have prevailed in Klein's family. Notwithstanding her penetrating analysis of the family in general, she appears out of touch with the terrible dilemma a parent and other family members might face with a child afflicted with a life-limiting illness. Her diagnosis of manic depression in Emmanuel may be correct but she misses the tragedy of his life situation and the melancholic effects of expectant death upon family members as well as the sense of guilt, helplessness and foreboding that this engenders.

In December 1902 Emmanuel travelled to Italy via Spain and his letters reflect a morbid, self-destructive state of mind. Grosskurth (1986, p. 35) speculates that by then he was addicted to the fatal combination of morphine and cocaine. Arriving in Genoa he found a note from Melanie to which he responded by postcard chiding her for its briefness. 'This scantiness has put me very much out of humour and still does so.' Unfortunately in a few hours he was dead – found slumped on a bed in his hotel room having suffered heart failure. Klein wrote in her memoir:

> He was twenty-five when he died. Here again [as with Sidonie] I have the feeling that, had one known more about medicine, one might have been able to do something to keep him alive longer . . . In my memory he remains a young, strong-minded man, as I knew him, strong in his opinions . . . with a deep understanding of art and a passion for it in many ways, and the best friend I ever had.
>
> (quoted from Grosskurth 1986, p. 19)

The reader is very aware that the comparison with Sidonie touches on the family's painful fears about health. In this instance, her brother did not spare Melanie any penitential guilt with his rebuke of 'scantiness' just before he died.

Depression in marriage and childbirth

Following her marriage in 1903 to Arthur Klein, a chemical engineer, Klein fell pregnant and a daughter Melitta was born into the couple's new home in Rosenberg, a small town in Switzerland. In her memoir she recounts that she threw herself into motherhood but in an unhappy state of mind, helpless to find a way out. One wonders about her state of mind given that she was still in mourning for Emmanuel.

Three years later, during and after her next pregnancy, Melanie suffered a major depression. In 1907 her son Hans was born. The family then moved to Krappitz, a small town in Poland where Arthur had secured a lucrative job. At this point Klein's mother, Libussa, moved from Vienna to take charge of the household. This only accelerated Klein's slide into a deeper depression, which Libussa tried to manage by exhorting her to visit friends and seek quiet places to relax and rest. This meant that Klein spent a large part of her two years in Krappitz away from home and away from her new baby – undergoing spa treatments and prolonged trips in search of sea air. These absences must have exacerbated anxieties already existing in the family about health. Furthermore, they may well have also heightened the already tense relationship between husband and wife that had been made worse by Melanie's discovery that Arthur had had an affair.

In spite of these various 'cures' and the regimes suggested by Libussa, Klein's symptoms never receded and eventually in May 1909 she was hospitalized for two and a half months. She was then moved to another clinic in St Moritz where her condition worsened due to a bladder infection. Her mother, understandably, was beside herself and suspected a pregnancy. Towards the end of that year Arthur was transferred to an even smaller town and such was Melanie's distress about this move that for her sake he arranged a transfer to Budapest instead. The establishment of a new home in a cosmopolitan city brought a remission of symptoms that lasted for the next two years. However, near the end of 1913 Klein was pregnant again and the spectre of depression, given her previous experience of childbirth, hung over the family afresh. In July 1914 another son, Erich, entered the household and Klein promptly employed a wet nurse.

But this time it was Melanie's mother who fell ill; within a few months of fading away she died on 6 November 1914. That put paid to Melanie's recovery from depression, but at least this was the city of Budapest, and it would be in Budapest that Melanie Klein began her association with Ferenczi, as analyst and supporter.

Grosskurth (1986) is unwavering in her view that it was the intrusive, over-solicitous, guilt-inducing presence of her mother in Melanie's married life that trapped her into her depressions. An extremely unflattering portrait of a smothering, divisive, jealous and undermining figure flies off the page that is in stark contrast to the picture of her mother that Klein herself presented in her memoir. This time, however, I think Grosskurth (1986: Chapter 3) diagnoses the situation correctly. She pinpoints the dynamic of ostensible self-sacrifice allied to a blame game that flourished among the family members. She recounts from Klein's memoir her memory of being at her mother's deathbed, and being taught how to make chicken soup, which Libussa then forced herself to eat in Melanie's presence. Klein concluded, probably innocently but somewhat disingenuously, that her mother was attempting to go on living for her sake. (Grosskurth 1986, p. 65).

Who can dictate, let alone judge, how someone should feel, or how he or she should behave, at a parent's deathbed? Yet Klein seems aware that this gesture of chicken soup was more than just a gift. She is quoted as feeling left 'with a feeling of guilt that I might have done more for her, and we know that such feelings exist. I knelt down by her bed and asked for forgiveness' (Grosskurth 1986, p. 64).

The 'other' side of love, guilt and reparation

I would suggest that the 'blame game' that Grosskurth alludes to is one of masochistic mothering where inexhaustible giving comes with a debt attached. The debt is a demand to be needed that replaces a wish to provide for the actual needs of the other and the result is a pull into a codependent relationship. In asking for her mother's forgiveness Klein suggests that what was given could never be repaid, yet the giving contained within it is an implicit expectation of reciprocation.

Furthermore, the guilt is reinforced when the mother becomes fragile, ill, or complains about her own aches and pains in the course of her mothering or grandmothering. In fact, there are several citations by Grosskurth (1986, pp. 29, 46, 57) of occasions when Libussa would complain of her own stomach aches when the children were ill. To top it off, any natural protest on the part of the child must be stifled lest the child appears churlish or ungrateful. In watching her mother choke the soup down, how could Klein not feel she had been a lifelong burden to her mother? And how could she not feel she would never be able to repay her?

I believe this pattern was laid down in the family through the expectation of premature child death. Both Sidonie and Emmanuel had low life expectancies owing to illnesses and therefore made the ultimate sacrifice of a shortened life that was not of their own choosing. This usually has a profoundly painful effect on family members, perhaps more so when the father is a general practitioner. Melanie was only 4 years old when the ailing Sidonie finally died, but she never forgot the 'gifts' bequeathed to her by her sister before her death. Emmanuel made Melanie believe he was her best friend. He shared all his intimate thoughts and experiences with her, especially his complaints about other family members. In return he expected her full devotion and love and where this was lacking he could 'twist the knife' (Grosskurth 1986, pp. 27–31). Her engagement to Arthur Klein, for example, brought out a nasty, jealous steak in him. Grosskurth provides ample examples through his letters of his possessiveness and his attempts to put her off her marriage. Emmanuel wrote from Venice:

> Do I need to repeat to you, that I have concentrated all the love and tenderness that I am capable of, and which I need to cherish in myself, on you and Mother . . . And that no greater and devastating disaster could befall me than to lose one of you in any way.
>
> (Grosskurth 1986, p. 34)

This is indeed a twisted communication. By emphasizing the disaster that would befall *him* should he be deserted by his mother and beloved sister, he plays upon the disastrous consequences for them if something untoward should happen to him. Is this not a message meant for beyond the grave? Such an obligation could surely be manageable only through massive idealization, but there would be no escape from the sense of a lifelong debt. Unless, that is, you too fell into a similar practice of self-sacrifice in your own life as a means of securing attachments of loyalty. This is the other side of love, guilt and reparation that Klein wrote little about.

Like Freud, Klein played a similar guilt trip on some of her colleagues in her later life, especially if she felt they were wavering in their total support. She would imply that she had endeavoured so hard on their behalf, sacrificed so much, brought them so far – how then could they now consider showing their gratitude by branching off into something else or pursuing some independent line of thought? Weren't they not simply being unthankful and churlish? Wilfred Bion himself, during his analysis with Klein, suffered under this regime over his interest in group work. He once told J. D. Sutherland that he had the impression that Klein was 'out of sympathy', perhaps even hostile, to his work on groups, with the implication that he was diverting his attention from more serious work (Sutherland 1985, p. 55).

Of course, Bion had his own problems concerning mother guilt, as we shall discover in Chapter 15, but there is a wonderful account by him in a letter to his wife at the time of attending the 1955 Geneva Congress with Klein and other colleagues (Bleandonu 1994, p. 104). Klein was very friendly to him – even sympathizing about his missing his wife – yet she expected him to spend time in her company. However, an excruciated Bion describes himself chafing under the burden of this demand by the 'head of school' when he desperately needed sleep. Interestingly, Bion complains of Klein's demands in the same way he complained about his mother's demands when in adult life she tried to communicate with him. It seems that he never forgave his mother for his 'sacrifice' of being sent at an early age to boarding school in England, and he later compounded matters by perceiving her subsequent attempts at restoration as signs of further burdensome claims upon him, and his adult achievements. This makes for an intriguing speculation as to how analyst and patient negotiated the maternal transference in terms of their respective inclinations to project guilt under the guise of self-sacrifice.

Death of Abraham and the rejection by Kloetzel

Springtime in Berlin. The year is 1925. Klein had moved there with her son Erich while she and her husband Arthur were considering a divorce. She joined the Berlin Society and in February 1923 was elected a full member, following which she entered analysis with Karl Abraham. She joined a dance class and fell unexpectedly in love with her dance partner, a married man named Chezkel Kloetzel. Apparently he bore a striking resemblance to her brother Emmanuel but the secret name they concocted for him was that of her first son Hans! The affair is well documented by Grosskurth (1986, pp. 141–150) from Klein's pocket book diary and a series of letters they wrote to one another.

These letters reveal genuine expressions of affection and love in both directions. However, by June of that year the affair appeared to be faltering. 'Depression' is the header in her diary under which Klein records the gradual falling apart of the relationship. In late July Kloetzel, who was travelling by sea, wrote to her announcing he had fallen in love with someone on the ship. When he arrived home he requested Klein find a new dance partner if she intended to continue with the classes. Klein was shattered but as the rejected one, she tried her best in her written responses to keep her composure in negotiating a way out, with all the painful lapses and veiled recriminations that occur at times like this. Kloetzel, for his part, used his upcoming assignment in Cape Town, South Africa to disentangle himself completely. Yet they may have kept in touch because in 1933 Kloetzel came to London looking for work, but when this failed to materialize he emigrated to Palestine.

To compound Klein's misery her analyst Abraham became ill at this time, seeing patients only when he was well enough. Within five months, however, at the end of 1925, he died, causing shock waves throughout the analytic community. A particularly painful aspect for Klein was that she had been analysing his two young sons.

In chronicling so far the sequence of events in Melanie Klein's life from the time she was 4 years old to December 1925 one cannot but reflect, in terms of loss and grief, how relentlessly calamitous and ill-fated her life had been up to this juncture. Though it was only brief, her affair with Kloetzel inspired an eruption of happiness in what had otherwise become a very gloomy terrain indeed – marked by continuous experiences of expectant death, actual loss and mourning. Would she ever be free of sorrow? Was she perhaps jinxed? Would there be any salvation? Apparently, yes – she had already begun to give a series of lectures in London, where she would eventually settle following an invitation by Ernest Jones to analyse his children. There she would go on to become a leading, if controversial, figure. Sadly, however, this move would not spare her from yet another tragedy that would once more claw away the scar tissue.

The death of Hans

In 1934, seven years after moving to London, Klein's second child Hans was living in what is now northern Slovakia near Ružomberok (Town of the Roses). There he was employed as an engineer in a paper factory. This town is significant on several accounts. As a young boy Hans attended a boarding school located in the Tatra Mountains, near Ružomberok. At that time he was also analysed by his mother during the school holidays (in Berlin) and he appears as 'Felix' in a case study (Klein 1932, Chapter 2).

Returning to Ružomberok, however, as an adult man, by coincidence or unconscious design, had the most fateful result for Hans. In piecing together the story, Grosskurth (1986, p. 214) relates how while out on a walk in the Tatra Mountains, the path gave way and he fell to his death. He was 27 years old, virtually the same age as Emmanuel. Klein could not attend the funeral in Budapest because she was too overcome. Like Emmanuel, Hans died alone and similar speculations grew about the nature of his death – was it an accident or suicide? Inexorably, Klein lapsed into another depression and while her supporters denied it was a clinical depression, there was a great deal of concern about her (Grosskurth 1986, pp. 218–219). She had a safety net, however, having earlier that year entered into analysis with Sylvia Payne.

With this loss it can be surmised that Klein probably faced the most terrible accumulation of sorrow and self-reproach. Although her home was now in England, she must have been plunged back into the past. It was during and after her pregnancy with Hans that she suffered her first severe depression. In search of rest, on her mother's urging, she was away from her children sometimes for weekly intervals. She had missed Hans's first birthday. Then there was all the countless family uprootings determined by Arthur's job and Melanie's health. These events punctuated by the strains that were already in the marriage eventually led to divorce.

It may well have been the burden of guilt over these inconsistent circumstances that stirred Klein's concern about the mental health of both Melitta and Hans and that persuaded her to later analyse them. Child analysis at that time consisted principally of assessing the nature of any problems and laying down a prophylactic base. In her husband's critical eyes, however, she had 'experimented' on Hans, though this accusation has an ironic edge. When we scrutinize her analysis of Hans (alias the 'Felix' case) we discover that when the father returned from his long business trips, he was cruel towards his son, contributing in no uncertain way to his symptoms. By analysing her children, however, in an atmosphere of marital strife, Klein ran the risk of perpetuating the example of her mother – of providing a guilt-based, over-solicitous attention that creates a sense of obligation owing to a debt attached. Perhaps this explains something of what was played out explosively with her daughter Melitta, who like her mother became an analyst – and not a lay analyst – who refused her mother's 'chicken soup' publicly, and was determined to feel no guilt or shame about it.

Conclusion

Klein suffered from depressive episodes that were welded to life events like repeated loss and disappointment as well as lifecycle events like pregnancy, which meant that her depressions took on an inexorable pattern and quality owing to the rekindling of previous depressions. The foundation was laid down by the death of her sister Sidonie when she was 4 years old. Although her father died when she was a teenager, she was less traumatized by his death. Thereafter the triggers for acute phases of depression were life events such as her experiences of childbirth, the loss of her beloved Emmanuel, her mother's death, the death of her analyst Abraham, her terrible rejection in love, and the tragic death of her son Hans.

Her first pregnancy and the birth of her first child, which led to depression, took place in the swift wake of Emmanuel's death. The child, being a baby girl, may well have revived the memory and loss of Sidonie. Then a complete depressive breakdown accompanied the birth of her next child, Hans. With the fortunate move to Budapest, however, there was a softening of depression only to be undone by the death of her mother.

Then another chance for recovery beckoned by going into analysis with Abraham, an expert on depression, yet this too abruptly ended with his death. Just as the recovery from one loss seemed underway, another one interceded. Consider, for instance, her disastrous affair with Kloetzel. This too was begun as part of her revival in Berlin, but it ended in a terrible, unkind rejection. Was the affair's demise foreshadowed in some way by the fact that Kloetzel resembled her brother Emmanuel, the great love of her life? Or that he was bizarrely given the secret name of Hans? Perhaps in its most pernicious form, depression operates in a premonitory way, like a web that draws calamities ineluctably to itself, resembling Freud's idea of a 'fate neurosis' where an illness craves to be fed by calamity in order to reproduce itself.

What role did Klein's depression play in her creative output and in the direction of her theoretical explorations? There can be no doubt that Klein, like many writers and artists, must have written from personal experience, but the question is whether her personal experience of depression helped her to develop new ideas and concepts? Grosskurth (1986, p. 215) claims that she wrote her best papers while suffering and that her work was her salvation. In other words, in her writing on subjects like grief, manic depression, guilt and reparation she was able to sublimate her agony in a way that not only enabled her to cope with depression but to achieve new insights into these subjects. This seems true for the period before and following Hans's death when she was seeing Sylvia Payne professionally.

During this period of maximal depression Klein (1935) wrote one of her most acclaimed papers – 'A contribution to the psychogenesis of manic-depressive states' – and undoubtedly her personal experiences must have contributed to her theme. The curiously modest title 'A contribution . . .' belies its ground-breaking content, both from the point of view of Klein's own theories and object relations theory generally. Also striking is the relatively sober opening soon followed by a cascade of intense writing that sweeps the reader along. The intensity is created by the many italicized passages that give the reader a thrilling sense of the writer urgently trying to convey new or improved ideas. The descriptions of mania, in particular, carry this degree of intensity where, almost resembling the subject, the reader has to keep up with the flow of ideas.

One wonders how Klein's peers, who obviously knew of her loss, responded when she presented this paper at the Lucerne Congress in August of 1934, merely three and a half months after Hans's death. Much of this energy in the paper, however, is directed towards proposing a more coherent theoretical structure with the concept of a universal infantile depressive position as its centrepiece. Depression, Klein declared, runs throughout the lifecycle and has its roots in mental struggles stretching back to infancy which, if not overcome developmentally, replicate themselves in a modified form in the mature person. If she were speaking from personal experience then her conception of a substrate for depression throughout the lifecycle would be entirely consistent with her experience.

Some of her personal experience of Hans's death would appear in a barely disguised form five years later in her paper 'Mourning and its relation to manic-depressive states' (1940) as highlighted by Pedder (1987). This took the form of a case study describing the recovery process during the mourning of a mother for her son.

> Mrs A, in the first few days after the shattering loss of her young son, who had died suddenly while at school, took to sorting out letters, keeping his and throwing others away. She was thus unconsciously attempting to restore him and keep him safe inside herself, and throwing out what she felt to be indifferent, or rather hostile.
>
> (Klein 1935, p. 323)

Mrs. A's reaction was initially one of emotional numbness with few tears and a cessation of dreaming. Then a dream materialized in which the dreamer felt hostile towards a mother in a black dress expecting the death of her son. The dream brought forth memories of Mrs. A's earlier life as a child and about her relationship with a talented older brother who had also died young. Through the dream it is discovered that alongside her love and admiration for this brother, she was also jealous of him and of his relationship with their mother. In fact, defensively, the dream then refers to the pairing of Mrs. A's own mother and the loss of her son and not Mrs. A's current loss. Two reactions result – empathy with the mother who lost a son and triumph over the brother and his special link to the mother. But this understanding of the dream ushers in an important insight for Mrs. A – that her death wishes towards her brother were disguising similar feelings for her own son. It is these feelings she must deal with in order to overcome deeper aspects of her grief. Hence the analytic process in the case reflects how Klein's own loss of her son Hans reawakened the loss of Emmanuel and how in overcoming the loss in the present necessitates working through features of previous losses. In other words, in recovering from present loss the adult is not reinstating the 'object' for the first time, and that such a reinstatement enables the rebuilding the inner world as a whole – which characterizes the successful work of mourning. These are the critical conclusions of the paper.

In summary, the total theory of the infantile depressive position is not only a theory of pathology but also a theory of health. Alongside Klein's familiar emphasis on anxiety, aggression, fragmentation, guilt, schizo-paranoid mechanisms, object loss and envy she also placed concepts such as the good object, integration, symbol formation, epistemophilia, hope, reparation and the capacity for enjoyment and gratitude at the heart of her theorizing. Interestingly, these latter concepts do not necessarily coincide with periods in her life when she was either her happiest or at her most creative. By extrapolation, therefore, it would probably be too simplistic to equate her writings on depression solely with periods of emotional turmoil and unhappiness. Her habit of theorizing in a dialectical way was distinctive and surprisingly modern – circularizing her argument, whatever subject she was discussing, by going back and forth between subject to object, between internal to external, between libido and aggression and so on in a way that sometimes tied the reader in knots. Characteristically, her most controversial concept of primary envy, her last major theoretical concept, took as its central theme the *good* object, showing a fatal attraction between illness and health. And when she wrote her final published paper 'On the sense of loneliness' (1963) she seemed at peace with her loss-ridden and turbulent past and could explain how inner loneliness, that is most pronounced during mental illness, can be relieved by turning to real relationships with the world, though never decisively.

Chapter 15

Bion's depression

For although the body dies the soul shall live forever.
I hope not with all my heart I hope not.

Wilfred Bion (1986)

Sometime in February 1959 while travelling on the London Underground, Bion fainted; his biographer Gerard Bleandonu (1994) diagnosed this as a return 'to the depression that continued to haunt him'. Heart disease and diabetes were ruled out and he was put on a diet and given a period of convalescence during which he worked on a paper titled 'Attacks on linking' (Bion 1959). Soon, however, he was beset with doubts about his work – 'I am at the moment feeling depressed about my paper, wondering if it's all just working around stalking a most majestic mare's nest' (Bion 1985, p. 129). This brings to mind Freud's similar bouts of depression about the quality of his work following difficult events in his life.

It is noteworthy that this is the sole reference in Bleandonu's biography to a tendency in Bion of depression yet in contemplating the string of adverse events in his lifestory one cannot escape the impression that statistically, to say the least, such a tendency would have been a natural response to these events. It is these events that I shall be canvassing in this exploration of Bion's depression, and I have chosen the following events, probably familiar to the many readers and admirers of Bion, to shed some light on what Bleandonu meant by 'the depression that continued to haunt him' – his exile from India at the age of 8 to attend public school in England; his experiences in two world wars; his rejection by his first fiancée; the death of his first wife following the birth of his first daughter; his ambivalent relationship with all his mentors and analysts that I would like to link to transference themes.

Schoolboy misery

At the age of 8 Bion was sent by his parents from India, where he was born and raised, to Bishop's Stortford College on the eastern outskirts of

Greater Edwardian London. The year was 1906 and his mother accompanied him on the long rail and sea journey. In his autobiography he describes their farewell at the school as follows:

> Thus when I found myself in the playground . . . where I kissed my mother a dry-eyed goodbye, I could see, above the hedge which separated me from her and the road which was the boundary of the wide world itself, her hat go bobbing up and down like some curiously wrought millinery cake carried on the wave of green hedge. And then she was gone.
>
> (Bion 1986, p. 33)

He recollects the 'numbed, stupefied' impact this had upon him. Recalling later his relationship with his mother, he described her as 'frightening' when it came to emotion. She was 'peculiar'.

> It felt queer if she picked me up and put me on her lap, warm and safe and comfortable. Then suddenly cold and frightening, as it was many years later at the end of school service when the doors were opened and a cold draught of night air seemed to sigh gently through the sermonically heated chapel.
>
> (Bion 1986, p. 9)

In contrast, the father of his childhood was not only venerated as a sensitive, compassionate man, but also lionized as a big game hunter who organized tiger hunts with royalty. The weight of this image bore down on the young boy one day during a railway journey with his father. They discovered a tiger trap that used as its bait a live young goat. Bion immediately identified with the goat and became upset – then he felt crushed by failing to live up to the ideal of the fearless father.

He found his new school a 'ghastly', 'gloomy' place. He spent his first night pulling the bedclothes over his head and crying himself to sleep. He felt the contrast between India and England most acutely: he hated the monotonous drizzle and longed for the heat and dust intensity of the Punjab where during the monsoon fierce rain would be followed by bright sunshine. His internal climate was under attack too and he made strenuous efforts to fight off this inner gloom. He felt particularly worn down by the tedium and pressure of the school day and he treasured being alone in bed at the end of the day. Yet there too he was tormented by loneliness, misery, bitterness and feelings of being deserted by his parents. For relief he gave himself over to masturbation, which since the age of 5 he had named 'wiggling' after he had experienced intense genital pleasure from lying face down on the floor and 'wiggling'. For all the boys, Bion claimed, 'wiggling' became the 'only redeeming thing' during this appalling period of their lives (Bion 1986, p. 47).

Bion's mother visited him several times at boarding school, but when she inquired if he was unhappy, he denied any loneliness or homesickness and suggested instead that he 'liked' the school. This might well have been retaliation for the time when it was first announced he was going to be schooled in England. At that time Bion became aware of his mother's sadness, but when he asked, 'You aren't sad are you?' she replied, 'Of course not! Why should I be sad?' (Bion 1986, p. 21). A lie could be reciprocated with another lie. She had denied any emotional loss and he would pay her back with the same. In answer to her question, instead of unburdening himself, he held it all in, believing that his mother couldn't take it. On his distress at night he commented ironically that he had learned to weep silently until 'I became like my mother, who was *not* laughing and *not* crying' (Bion 1986, p. 34).

One can only speculate how this perception of his mother's denial of emotion so early on influenced his later ideas about 'containment' as depicted in the following passage from 'Attacks on linking':

> Projective identification makes it possible for [the patient] to investigate his own feelings in a personality powerful enough to contain them. Denial of the use of this mechanism, either by refusal of the mother to serve as a repository for the infant's feeling, or by hatred and envy of the patient who cannot allow the mother to exercise this function, leads to the destruction of the link between infant and the breast and consequently to a severe disorder of the impulse to be curious on which all learning depends.
>
> (Bion 1959, pp. 106–107)

Of course Bion, in the same manner, would later subject the psychoanalytic community to a similar test. Through his dense writing style, coupled with his often arcane subject matter, he probed the community to see whether they could absorb his ideas receptively, or whether they would call them 'mad' and allow no ingress of them into the psychoanalytic corpus. Bion wrote about this in his analysis of the mystic.

Your country needs YOU!

In no less than six months following his completion of school, just before his eighteenth birthday, Bion faced another tense separation from his parents. After a failed first attempt to enlist, he joined the armed forces with his father's help in January 1916 to participate in what became known as the Great War – so-called because of the heinous number of casualties. This would be the war that Freud's sons Martin and Ernst would also see

action in, though on the opposite side. The swift transition from the institution of school to the institution of the army brought with it similar fears
and familiar conflicts for the sensitive and perspicacious Bion. The cold, the
wet, the fog, the ubiquitous mud and the interminable waiting for something to happen, was probably reminiscent of those monotonous Sundays
at school – but this time there was the stench of death.

Bion saw action as a junior officer in Belgium Flanders as a tank driver.
He chronicled his experiences and reflections in war memoirs *The Long
Weekend* written directly after the Armistice (Bion 1986). In this memoir,
which is the first of his autobiographical series, he describes his participation in the battle of Cambrai – a momentous event in his young life. His
tank was badly hit by a shell and his crew and some infantrymen managed
to secure their position in a German trench. They counterattacked until
their ammunition ran out, at which time they were joined by a company of
Seaforth Highlanders. When the commander was shot through the head,
Bion was asked to take over the company temporarily.

Bion was hailed as a hero and recommended for the Victoria Cross.
While he denied any personal bravery he accepted the two awards made to
him – the Distinguished Service Order, followed by the Légion d'honneur.
At the end of the war he attended an investiture at Buckingham Palace,
where his mother was waiting for him outside. Here unfolded a familiar
awkward scene between the passively hostile son who by now bridled at any
sign of affection from his exasperated mother. In a sarcastic biographical
note Bion claimed that it had been a shame that his mother had not
witnessed the award ceremony personally because the 'glorious moment'
was so much more for her than for him (Bion 1986, p. 190). Making light of
a mother's relief and pleasure at her son having survived the war, let alone
being honoured, seems particularly unkind given what it leaves out – the
distress and helplessness faced by mothers who were forced to endure their
sons going off to war, in Bion's case, so eagerly. He implies that his mother
would have derived some narcissistic 'benefit' from his terrible sacrifice
during the war – perhaps in the same way, in his eyes, she had 'benefited'
from his school career at his most hated boarding school. His dedication of
his war memoir to his mother could be understood in the context of this
militant type of bitterness.

Evidence of his deep grievance characteristically emerged during fare-
wells. A few weeks following the investiture, mother and son were faced
with yet another goodbye prior to his return to France. 'It was simply a
matter of compelling our face muscles to do their drill' is how Bion describes
their turgid interaction before making his way to Waterloo Station (Bion
1986, p. 191). In another train-window departure scene several months later,
with similar moroseness, he made it clear he wanted nothing more than to
get back to the Front and to get away from her: 'I can only hope she had a
similar wish to be rid of me' (Bion 1986, p. 266). He had clearly not forgiven

his mother for her role in his exile from India, and particularly for suppressing her sadness and replacing it with false emotion. Now he would be the leaver, not the left, in order to transmit to her, via a mechanism (projective identification) he would become famous for in describing in psychotic states of mind, his own past feelings of shock and abandonment. Hostility towards a needed yet disappointing parent has often been associated with depression (Jacobson 1971).

In his own account of the war it is obvious that Bion (1986) was profoundly haunted by his terrible and cruel ordeal. He mentions every serviceman's harrowing exposure to carnage and every serviceman's expectation of death. Before leaving for the Front, he divided all his precious books and personal effects among his friends. Having survived a full year of bedlam, he questioned whether he had 'exhausted [his] quota of chances of survival' (Bion 1986, p. 247). He mentions too the horror of exposure to being 'under fire' and the actual injuries of men 'shot to bits' from which there was little respite. He mentions how with so many deaths it was impossible to form attachments without anticipating they would be severed and replaced by new faces. Then there was Bion's fear of losing his mind, described in experiences of dissociation – losing interest in life, descending into hopelessness, looking forward to being killed. At times Bion's invective about the officer/soldier system paralleled his condemnation of the barbarity of the boarding school system where 'Masters and boys alike were caught up in a web which we did not see even as we struggled to free ourselves' (Bion 1986, p. 92).

His biographer Bleandonu (1994) speculates about the correlation between Bion's war experiences and the themes and concepts he would later develop and focus on in his work – themes such as the experience of intolerable emotions, the theme of truth and lies, the concept of 'nameless dread'. One could add that given he had not succumbed to a total mental breakdown, particularly during the Great War, this may have formed his belief that in such a breakdown the psychotic's ego is never completely withdrawn from reality. The following statement too could be read as an emotional assessment by Bion of someone having come through the ravages of war: 'They say animals are aware of the imminence of an earthquake. Humans are sensitive to the imminence of an emotional upheaval' (Bion 1979, p. 102).

Interestingly, Bion describes his friendship with one young man Quainton, who one day suddenly went on leave without returning. Some months later he contacted his battalion to explain that he had been in car accident and had been subsequently admitted to a mental hospital with a diagnosis of 'shell shock'. Throughout Bion's own account, as well as in Bleandonu's biography, there is nothing more than a passing suggestion that Bion himself might have suffered from shell-shock. Yet when he enrolled at Queen's College Oxford following the war to study history, he was plagued by nightmares from which he would wake drenched in sweat. The themes of these nightmares were usually war related and on waking they left him with the impression of going crazy (Bion 1985, p. 16).

Bion completed his degree in 1921, but he was thwarted from entering academic life by missing out on an honours degree because of late registration. Instead he went in search of a job and landed up at the most improbable place – his hated school at Bishop's Stortford. In his two years there he became a popular teacher and sports master, but then one day he was summarily fired. The hapless Bion had been accused by a mother of sexual advances towards her son. In shock he was thrown back onto his schoolboy guilt surrounding his sexuality issues and he did not contest the case (Bleandonu 1994, p. 37).

Rejected in love

Perhaps it is not coincidental that this section deals with the trauma of romantic rejection. This occurred at the time when Bion was in his late twenties and well ensconced in his medical studies to become a surgeon but with no certain financial security. He met a young woman, who responded to his attentions by sending him a box of wild roses, a gesture that completely overwhelmed him. He wrote back and they met from time to time in London where Bion proposed marriage and was accepted. A few weeks later she broke off the engagement by letter, leaving Bion in a state of shock. Had she not vowed eternal fidelity? In his autobiography this shock and disappointment is mentioned several times with considerable rancour. He focuses on the meaning of the roses and the terrible betrayal, especially when he discovered she had been in love with someone else all along. He also recounts running into her some time later in a seaside town with the other man. She offered him an apple, probably as a sort of gesture of reconciliation – but Bion's blood was up and he felt murderous. He regretted not having his service revolver with him to shoot the man. 'Then I would have shot her through the knee in such a way that the joint could not be repaired' (Bion 1985, p. 30). The experience of being drawn in and dropped, must have been a painful echo of his mother's ability to be warm and then suddenly cold. But the Oedipal dimension rings out too in the tableau centred on the 'mother' as whore whose betrayal can never be forgiven.

It was at this time, while studying medicine, that Bion sought psychotherapy. His apparent reason was to gain help in understanding his anxieties about his academic and sporting disappointments at Oxford (Bleandonu 1994, p. 41). In his autobiographical account Bion is quite scornful of his therapist whom he dubbed Dr FiP, that is, 'Dr Feel-it-in-the-past'. Even though he stayed for six years, he criticized Dr FiP's method of relating present difficulties to some past trauma, and he took particular exception to one interpretation that suggested that after his abandonment by his fiancée he had fallen 'back on himself'. By all accounts Dr FiP was working analytically and, although we have no way of knowing, it seems likely that he was referring to Bion's use of masturbation to console himself against loss. Certainly by this stage in his therapy the manifest reasons for seeking treatment had given way to analysis of more personal issues relating to the past, including sexuality issues. However, in writing about it years later he continued with his caricature, 'If your girl runs away with a rival today, don't worry, but feel it in the past' (Bion 1985, p. 35). It is the analyst, it seems, in the mother transference, who eschews empathy.

In the end however, it seemed that Dr FiP could not be squared in Bion's mind with the idealized picture of the father as the tiger hunter. There would be other senior male figures too in his life that would suffer a similar fate. At the time Bion complained about his difficulties in meeting therapy payments and how Dr FiP let him run up a large debt. Again he suggests that in return for his hard endeavours to improve himself and keep himself afloat all that he received in return was inept environmental support. There would be similar complaints about fees during his analysis with Melanie Klein. For instance, he regarded it as monstrous that she charged him for sessions when he was ill. The finale with Dr FiP arrived when he referred a young patient to Bion. This immediately aroused Bion's suspicion of some kind of impropriety: he suspected a fee-splitting association was being proposed, even though the therapist denied this. Nevertheless, he leapt at the opportunity, took the high moral ground, and terminated his therapy. This was clearly a type of acting out. Was it something to do with the 'impropriety' Bion had been accused of by his *alma mater* before they terminated his employment?

These recollections appear in a book titled *All My Sins Remembered and The Other Side of Genius* (Bion 1985). Such a title initially sounds playfully ironic, even self-mocking, but the intention was to show not only the bad and ugly but also the good side of Bion. Nonetheless, in the first section no attempt is made to disguise the depth of his bitterness and resentment about certain periods in his past. Even though Bion's aim is to bare his 'sins', the tone of his writing fails to evoke any sense of the author's capacity for forgiveness of others. It also leaves the reader questioning his reluctance to acknowledge when his objects had actually been helpful to him. The two exceptions are his *ayah* – his childhood nanny in India, whom he recalled with affection – and his second wife Francesca. The letters to Francesca and his daughter brim over with affection and joy, but they also reveal his vulnerability and strong dependency needs. He was later to have two children by this marriage, Julian, and Nicola when Bion was 58 years old. However, what emerges is a clear split between the past and the present with little recognition given to how his sense of isolation in struggling with his life challenges had contributed to his general ambivalence towards internal objects.

Another war, a deeper loss

In 1939 England was at war again and Bion signed up dutifully. In the meantime he had completed his medical training at University College London, joined the Tavistock Clinic, and in 1937 started a training analysis with John Rickman that lasted for two years until the war began. Rickman came with impeccable credentials, having been analysed by Freud, Ferenczi and Melanie Klein. However, in his new analysis the same old ambivalence about the 'feeling-it-in-the-past' approach emerged and this must have been exacerbated by the fact that his mother died during this period. There is little information available, both biographically and autobiographically, about his reaction to her death. This may not be remarkable given Bion's persistently ambivalent attitude towards his mother. Yet he was present at her deathbed and described pithily, though with a certain ironic poignancy, her response to a vase of spring flowers on a table that had begun to wilt. 'I can hold them up no longer', she said. 'Will you hold them up for me?' (Bion 1986, p. 266).

While he was at University College he had met an actress Betty Jardine, and they were soon married. During the war Bion received various postings as a military psychiatrist where he tried to introduce new methodologies for army personnel, including the idea of treating soldiers nearer their units rather than in hospitals. As the war neared its end Wilfred and Betty were expecting their first baby. Then Bion accepted a final posting to Normandy, where he heard of the arrival of a baby daughter. Tragically, his wife Betty died three days later of a pulmonary embolism.

According to Bleandonu (1994), Bion never forgave himself for not being present at his child's birth. He also wonders whether this was not the greatest of Bion's 'Sins Remembered' in his biography. In one passage Bion cries, 'I had begged Betty to agree to have a baby: her agreement to do so had cost her life' (1985, p. 70). One simply cannot imagine the suffering of the man. His guilt was compounded by his belief that he had also deprived his daughter of a mother. Subsequently, he was released from service and settled in a small house outside London, where he employed a housekeeper to help him raise his daughter. In the year that followed, when he resumed his training as an analyst and focused on his group work, Bion was still in full mourning. To a colleague J. D. Sutherland he once said, 'You think you are out of it; then there is a day when everything brings it all back and you relive it again' (Sutherland 1985). But in the main, wrote Sutherland, Bion habitually kept his suffering to himself.

Bad, mad or sad

I am always hearing – as I have always done – that I am a Kleinian, that I am crazy. Is it possible to be interested in that sort of dispute?

(Bion 1992, p. 377)

Bion was rarely, if ever, given to self-praise and preferred self-parody. He described himself as timid, morose and cowardly. 'My character, when I glimpsed it, was horrible – in contrast with my wishes' (Bion 1985, p. 214). Bleandonu (1994) puts this down to 'a narcissistic preoccupation tinged with guilt'. Some sort of moral failure indeed seems to be suggested in his comments that could account for a sense of inadequacy and self-disappointment; these are signature signs of depression.

In some ways Bion was forced into becoming the proverbial product of a boarding school education where beneath the appearance of a doughty independence there festered a great vulnerability that expressed itself through a litany of complaints about emotional hardship, neglect and rotten luck – that had to be endured. This neglect was then subsequently projected onto subsequent maturational environments. In Bion's case, these environments included teachers, institutions, fiancées and analysts that all seemed to fail him in some way. In *All My Sins Remembered*, he asks himself, 'How did you find out life?' In the plural he replies, 'They find out the hard way, by going to England to school, by not doing sexual things, by winning a military cross, by becoming independent, twenty-one, earning their own living and free to do whatever they like' (Bion 1985, p. 30). This brooding yet painful self-assessment rests on a combination of resentment, feeling unsupported and therefore unjustly burdened by life's undertakings.

At the height of his intellectual powers, in the decade between 1955 and 1965, when he had forged a new marriage and a new family, he seemed to have ultimately realized his longed-for desire of professional independence. This can be measured by the fact that in the years that followed all groupings within the British Society, the Kleinians, Independents and Contemporary Freudians, absorbed Bion's ideas, making possible a shared perspective on the relationship between the inside and the outside. This was the time he was happy, perhaps because he was getting something for himself. Internally, this environment meant he could be freer with himself without fear and resentment.

Bion's depression can be linked to his intense ambivalence towards his early love objects that persisted well into adult life. Bleandonu (1994, p. 277) highlights the fact that the later passages of his biography contain no references to his parents, suggesting that as an adult man Bion had virtually rendered himself parentless. This may have reflected his final triumph over the injustices of the past. However, his ambivalence towards his internal objects was rekindled every time he faced hardship and turmoil in the undertaking of 'finding out life'. Events such as his experience of boarding school, his participation in war, his losses and disappointments, and, like Freud, his worries about money and his struggle to establish himself professionally had burdened him terribly – and left a legacy of grievance combined with self-reproach.

His ambivalence was no less evident towards contemporary good objects, such as his analysts Dr FiP, James Hadfield, John Rickman and Melanie Klein. Even though he believed they all exhibited a kind of 'common sense' he nonetheless felt 'put upon' or trapped by them in different ways – with Dr FiP and Hadfield he mistrusted their focus on the child in the adult, with Rickman he seemed to imply his analyst had fallen in love with him and with Klein he was competitive and passed this off as a belief that she wanted him to develop in a particular direction. One gets the overriding impression that Bion easily felt imposed upon by people's systems of thought, especially if they manifested themselves in the form of pre-digested knowledge. To speculate, this may have been a driving factor in his attraction to inductive theories of mind that emphasized the less declamatory aspects of knowledge and more the discovery dimension to knowledge – a fragile and sometimes frustrating process for which claims of 'understanding' are always provisional – even when the frustration can be tolerated.

Descriptions by others of his personality were nonetheless revealing of a depressive dimension. He was variously depicted in epithets such as 'withdrawn', 'uncommunicative', 'laconic' 'brusque', 'gloomy', 'oversensitive to criticism', and so on. This is not to imply he had no wit; on the contrary he could be sardonic in the extreme, remarking one evening before a lecture he was about to give, 'I can hardly wait to hear what I have to say'. He certainly tended to exercise his wit masochistically rather than to attack others. To audiences he appeared recondite, cryptic, elliptical, impish and improvisational. He was also once described as coming at you 'from very far back in his head'. When you looked at him, however, at his 'set' facial expression, it was difficult not to think of depression. But what if Bion's search was a simple one – for an independent and ultimately private self in which he could keep his thoughts to himself and be altogether free to live the life he may have once imagined living as a child growing up in the twilight years of Imperialist India.

In leaving London in 1968 for Los Angeles he probably hoped for a respite from a life curve of unremitting responsibility, sacrifice and idealization – he had already been director of the London Clinic of Psychoanalysis, president of the British Psychoanalytic Society and had served on training and publication committees. He may, moreover, have dreamt of being finally released from the task of forging a life largely through his own endeavours. When he left England one significant speculation at the time was that he was escaping the burden of further leadership that might otherwise fall to him in the wake of Melanie Klein's death. But no such fate for the luckless Bion – while he enjoyed an initial period of anonymity in the City of Angels he soon found himself once again 'thrust into the role of a sort of messiah or deity' (Bion 1992, p. 376).

Notes

1 Depression today: a critical point in understanding and treatment

1 'Treatment as usual' means any treatment that patients are receiving from their primary care physician, including medication.
2 It is noteworthy that in spite of these comprehensive reviews regarding efficacy, CBT and computerized CBT (CCBT) interventions continue to be recommended in the revised UK NICE guidelines of 2007 for dysthymia, while for moderate or severe depression combination treatment of SSRIs and intensive psychological intervention (CBT or IPT) remain the principal recommendations. The 2009 press release, however, which updates treatment guidance, recommends a broader approach tailored to the individual.
3 These are deductions from the Tavistock Adult Depression Study, which has as its focus refractory depression. Principal Investigator: Professor Peter Fonagy (the previous Principal Investigator was Phil Richardson); Clinical Director: Dr David Taylor.

2 Freud's theory of depression

1 Melanie Klein (1934, p. 27) would later add that in suicide the subject achieves a double gain – he acts out his ambivalence towards the object while simultaneously ensuring that in the act of suicide he binds himself to the object forever.

4 Melanie Klein's theory of depression

1 'Lull', copyright © 1940 Theodore Roethke, from *Collected Poems of Theodore Roethke* by Theodore Roethke. Used by permission of Doubleday, a division of Random House Inc.
2 Enrique Pichon-Rivière (1971), the revered Argentinean analyst, advocated primary depression as a structure underlying all forms of psychopathology – he claimed that other symptoms are merely attempts at an elaboration of, or detachment from, this central situation.
3 This formulation of recycling explains how the melancholic never succeeds in setting up the lost object in the ego. It also illustrates how the obsessive and omnipotent nature of the narcissistic identification short-circuits the painful work of de-cathexis (Klein 1940, p. 350).

6 Winnicott on depression

1 Winnicott encounters a paradox here. While he states that clinical depression is not associated with the depressive position, he also states on the previous page, 'this is the first time I have linked the term depression with the depression position concept' (Winnicott 1954, p. 271).
2 As the poem at the beginning of the chapter suggests, Winnicott's mother suffered from depression.

7 A note on Fairbairn's concept of 'futility'

1 Rosenfeld's (1964) distinction between libidinal and destructive narcissism, while overlapping with Fairbairn's libidinal and anti-libidinal egos, is conceptually tied to Klein's notion of unconditional hatred.

8 Analytic subtypes of depression

1 See also Brown and Harris (1978) on the significance of self-esteem in depression.
2 It is noteworthy that in her last published paper, 'On the sense of loneliness', Klein (1963) wrote of an inner sense of loneliness that flows from an ubiquitous longing for an unattainable perfect internal state. She characterized this state as 'an unsatisfied longing for an understanding without words' (Klein 1963, p. 301).

9 A theoretical contribution to the problem of relapse

1 A better model would be one with a triangular as opposed to a bi-polar design, as proposed long ago by Whybrow and Mendels (1969). They characterized depression, mania and normal state as occupying the three vertices of the triangle with mixed-state depression occurring on the line segment between depression and mania. This model permits either state to revert to the normal without passing through the moods of the other vertices – which the authors explain accounts for the clinical fact that people can move from normal to mania and vice versa without getting depressed.
2 One can only but wonder whether the current over-diagnosis of bi-polar disorder in adolescents is attributable to an iatrogenic effect of SSRIs and whether an in-depth psychological assessment should be mandatory when diagnosing depression in this group. The finding by Martin et al. (2004) that a long-term exposure of adolescents to SSRIs increases the risk of conversion to bi-polar disorder seems to offer an explanation for the growing assumption in the mental health community that clinical forms of depression have a lifetime course.
3 While there are some parallels in theory between CBT and psychodynamic therapy (PDT), it is unlikely that they utilize the same underlying mechanisms or pathways for therapeutic change. In terms of clinical philosophy too, and the ethics of technique, there are unbridgeable differences. In PDT the emphasis is on following the patient instead of leading; allowing the evolution of goals; reaching after meaning and not trying to influence, and focusing on growth not change.

10 The correlation between dream work and the work of mourning

1 I believe this type of transformation can be a guide to the therapist of how far the unconscious work of mourning has come, because it reflects the stages necessary for the object to become an internal object.

12 The depressed child: the scandal of prescribing antidepressants

1 Longitudinal studies confirm that continuity between adolescent and adult depression begins in late adolescence (Lewinson et al. 1994).

2 In 2003 the US Food and Drug Administration (FDA) issued a health advisory warning on the risk of suicidal thinking in children taking antidepressants. The use of Prozac was the only SSRI passed by the FDA when considering the balance of risks and benefits to be favourable, although it was considered beneficial in only a minority of patients: the figure quoted was 1 in 10. Following the FDA warning the diagnosis and treatment of depression in children and adults dropped back to 1999 levels especially among paediatricians and primary care providers. (Libby et al. 2009).

3 Fairly common side-effects with the SSRIs include excitation, agitation, nausea, vomiting, diarrhoea, dizziness and chills. Less common side-effects include muscle twitching, fever, confusion, diaphoresis, seizures, delirium and coma (Kutcher 1997).

4 These results were confirmed by a similar study at Cambridge (Goodyer et al. 2007) in the same year using a combination of an SSRI and CBT together with clinical care.

5 For a thorough critique of the claims of this study, see Jureidini et al. (2004a); Jureidini et al. (2004b).

6 Questions about the effectiveness of short-term interventions for depression and their possible iatrogenic role in relapse are discussed in Chapter 9.

7 Centers for Disease Control and Prevention, National Center for Injury Prevention and Control. Web-based Injury Statistics Query and Reporting System (WISQARS): www.cdc.gov/injury/wisqars/index.html (accessed June 2009).

8 Healthy Place, America's Mental Health Channel: www.healthyplace.com/ (accessed August 2009).

13 Freud's depression

1 Freud's tremendous worry and depression about his sons and other relatives surviving the war was reignited during the Nazi occupation of Vienna in March 1938. This time the agony was focused on Anna when the Gestapo arrested her. Such was the anxiety and dread over possible torture and her general safety that Schur supplied her with Veronal, if suicide was called for. The twelve hours before she was released was pure torture for Freud and it was apparently this incident that finally convinced him to leave Vienna (Roazen 1972, p. 522). In departing he was asked by the authorities to confirm in writing that he had not been mistreated in any way. In signing the document he famously added, 'I can most highly recommend the Gestapo to everyone' (Gay 1995, p. 625).

2 As also reported by Jones (1957, III, p. 97) Freud later confided in Mary Bonaparte that since the boy's death he had never been able to be fond of anyone new, but merely retained his old attachments.

3 From the age of 37 he confessed he had lost interest in sex (Freud–Fliess Letters, 17 December 1896).

References

Abraham, H. C. and Freud, E. L. (1965). *The Letters of Sigmund Freud and Karl Abraham 1907–1926*. New York: Basic Books.

Abraham, K. (1911). Notes on the psycho-analytical investigation and treatment of manic-depressive insanity and allied conditions. In *Selected Papers of Karl Abraham*. London: Hogarth Press, 1927.

—— (1924). A short study of the development of the libido. In *Selected Papers of Karl Abraham*. London: Hogarth Press, 1927.

Abram, J. (2007). *The Language of Winnicott: A Dictionary of Winnicott's Use of Words*, 2nd edn. London: Karnac.

American Psychiatric Association (APA) (1994). *Diagnostic and Statistical Manual of Mental Disorders* (DSM-IV). Washington, DC: APA.

Anzieu, D. (1986). *Freud's Self-Analysis*. London: Hogarth Press and the Institute of Psychoanalysis.

Baumer, F. M., Howe, M., Gallelli, K., Simeonova, D. I., Hallmayer, J. and Chang, K. D. (2006). A pilot study of antidepressant-induced mania in pediatric bipolar disorder: Characteristics, risk factors, and the serotonin transporter gene. *Biological Psychiatry* 60, 1005–1012.

Beck, A. T. and Alford, B. A. (2009). *Depression: Causes and Treatment*, 2nd edn. Philadelphia, PA: University of Philadelphia Press.

Beck, A. T., Freeman, A. and Davis, D. D. (2004). *Cognitive Therapy of Personality Disorders*. New York: Guilford Press.

Bibring, E. (1953). The mechanism of depression. In P. Greenacre (ed.) *Affective Disorders*. New York: International Universities Press.

Bion, W. R. (1959). Attacks on linking. *International Journal of Psychoanalysis* 40, 5–6.

—— (1962). A theory of thinking. *International Journal of Psychoanalysis* 43, 306–310.

—— (1965). *Transformations*. London: Heinemann.

—— (1979). *A Memoir of the Future. Book Three: The Dawn of Oblivion*. Perthshire: Clunie Press.

—— (1985). *All My Sins Remembered and the Other Side of Genius*. Abingdon: Fleetwood.

—— (1986). *The Long Weekend*. London: Free Association Books.

—— (1992). *Cogitations*. London: Karnac.

Blatt, S. J. (1974). Levels of object representation in anaclitic and introjective depression. *Psychoanalytic Study of the Child* 29, 107–157.

Blatt, S. J. and Blass, R. B. (1992). Relatedness and self-definition: Two primary dimensions in personality development, psychopathology, and psychotherapy. In J. Barron, M. Eagle and D. Wolitsky (eds) *The Interface between Psychoanalysis and Psychology*. Washington, DC: American Psychological Association.

Blatt, S. J. and Ford, R. Q. (1994). *Therapeutic Change: An Object Relations Perspective*. New York: Plenum Press.

Blatt, S. J., D'Afflitti, J. P. and Quinlan, D. M. (1976). Experiences of depression in normal young adults. *Journal of Abnormal Psychology* 85, 383–389.

Blatt, S. J., Quinlan, D. M. and Chevron, E. (1990). Empirical investigations of a psychoanalytic theory of depression. In J. Masling (ed.) *Empirical Studies of Psychoanalytic Theories*, Vol. 3. Hillsdale, NJ: Analytic Press.

Blatt, S. J., Quinlan, D. M., Pilkonis, P. A. and Shea, T. (1995). Impact of perfectionism and need for approval on the brief treatment of depression: The National Institute of Mental Health Treatment of Depression Collaborative Research Program revisited. *Journal of Consulting and Clinical Psychology* 63, 125–132.

Blatt, S. J., Zuroff, D. C., Quinlan, D. M. and Pilkonis, P. (1996). Interpersonal factors in brief treatment of depression: Further analyses of the NIMH Treatment of Depression Collaborative Research Program. *Journal of Consulting and Clinical Psychology* 64, 162–171.

Bleandonu, G. (1994). *Wilfred Bion: His Life and Works, 1897–1979*. London: Free Association Books; New York: Guilford Press.

Bleichmar, H. (1996). Some subtypes of depression and their implications for psychoanalytic treatment. *International Journal of Psychoanalysis* 77, 935–961.

Bowlby, J. (1960). Grief and mourning in infancy. *Psychoanalytic Study of the Child* 17, 9.

—— (1980). *Attachment and Loss: Loss, Sadness and Depression*, Vol. 3. New York: Basic Books.

Brown, G. W. and Harris, T. (1978). *Social Origins of Depression: A Study of Psychiatric Disorder in Women*. London: Tavistock.

Burlingham, M. J. (1989). *The Last Tiffany: A Biography of Dorothy Tiffany Burlingham*. New York: Atheneum.

Centers for Disease Control and Prevention, National Center for Injury Prevention and Control. Web-based Injury Statistics Query and Reporting System (WISQARS). www.cdc.gov/injury/wisqars/index.html (accessed June 2009).

Chang, K. D. and Ketter, T. A. (2001). Special issues in the pharmacotherapy of paediatric bipolar disorder. *Expert Opinion in Pharmacotherapy* 2(4), 613–622.

Clark, A. F. (2004). Incidences of new prescribing by British child and adolescent psychiatrists: A prospective study over twelve months. *Journal of Psychopharmacology* 18, 115–120.

Clark, L. A. (2005). Temperament as a unifying basis for personality and psychopathology. *Journal of Abnormal Psychology* 114(4), 505–521.

Clark, R. W. (1982). *Freud: The Man and the Cause*. London: Paladin.

Cooper, J. and Murray, L. (1998). Postnatal depression. *British Medical Journal* 316, 1884–1886.

Corveleyn, J., Luyten, P. and Blatt, S. J. (eds) (2005). *The Theory and Treatment of*

Depression: Towards a Dynamic Interactionism Model. Leuven: Leuven University Press; Mahwah, NJ: Lawrence Erlbaum.

Deutsch, H. (1933). *The Psychology of Manic-Depressive States, with Particular Reference to Chronic Hypomania in Neuroses and Character Types.* New York: International Universities Press.

—— (1951). Abstract of panel discussion of mania and hypomania. *Bulletin of American Psychoanalytic Association* 7(3).

Elkin, I. (1994). The NIMH Treatment of Depression Collaborative Research Program. In A. E. Bergin and S. L. Garfield (eds) *Handbook of Psychotherapy and Behaviour Change*, 4th edn, pp. 114–142. New York: Wiley.

Eysenck, H. J. (1959). *Manual of the Maudsley Personality Inventory*. London: London University Press.

Eysenck, H. J. and Eysenck, S. B. (1975). *Manual of the Eysenck Personality Questionnaire*. London: Hodder and Stoughton.

Fairbairn, W. R. D. (1949). Steps in the development of an object-relations theory of the personality. In W. R. D. Fairbairn (1952) *Psychological Studies of the Personality*. London: Routledge and Kegan Paul.

—— (1952). *Psychological Studies of the Personality*. London: Routledge and Kegan Paul.

—— (1958). On the nature and aims of psychoanalytic treatment. *International Journal of Psychoanalysis* 39, 374–385.

Fava, G. A. (2002). Long-term treatment with antidepressant drugs: The spectacular achievements of propaganda. *Psychotherapy and Psychosomatics* 71, 127–132.

Fenichel, O. (1945). *The Psychoanalytic Theory of Neurosis*. New York: Norton.

Fonagy, P. (1991). Thinking about thinking: Some clinical and theoretical considerations in the treatment of a borderline patient. *International Journal of Psychoanalysis* 76, 39–44.

Freud, S. (1892). Melancholia: From pre-psychoanalytic publications and unpublished drafts. *S. E. 1*, 200–206.

—— (1900). *The Interpretation of Dreams. S. E. 4–5*.

—— (1905). *Three Essays on the Theory of Sexuality. S. E. 7*, 125–245.

—— (1911). Formulations on the two principles of mental functioning. *S. E. 12*, 218–226.

—— (1915a). Thoughts for the times on war and death. *S. E. 14*, 275–300.

—— (1915b). Instincts and their vicissitudes. *S. E. 14*, 111–140.

—— (1917). Mourning and melancholia. *S. E. 14*, 239–258.

—— (1920). Beyond the pleasure principle. *S. E. 18*, 7–64

—— (1921). Group psychology and the analysis of the ego. *S. E. 18*, 67–143.

—— (1925). Negation. *S. E. 19*, 235–239.

—— (1926). Inhibitions, symptoms and anxiety. *S. E. 20*, 87–174.

—— (1930). Civilization and its discontents. *S. E. 21*, 59–145.

—— (1933). *New Introductory Lectures to Psychoanalysis. S.E. 22*, 3–182.

Furman, E. (1974). *A Child's Parent Dies: Studies in Childhood Bereavement*. New Haven, CT: Yale University Press.

Gay, P. (1995). *Freud: A Life for our Time*. London: Macmillan.

Goodwin, F. K. and Jamison, K. R. (2007). *Manic-Depressive Illness: Bipolar Disorders and Recurrent Depression*, 2nd edn. New York: Oxford University Press.

Goodyer, I., Dubicka, B., Wilkinson, P., Kelvin, R., Roberts, C., Byford, S. et al.

(2007). Selective serotonin reuptake inhibitors (SSRIs) and routine specialist care with and without cognitive behaviour therapy in adolescents with major depression: Randomized controlled trial. *British Medical Journal* 335(7611), 142.

Grinstein, A. (1980). *Sigmund Freud's Dreams*, 2nd edn. New York: International Universities Press.

Grosskurth, P. (1986). *Melanie Klein: Her World and Her Work*. London: Maresfield Library.

Harrington, R. (2002). Affective disorders. In M. Rutter and E. Taylor (eds) *Child and Adolescent Psychiatry: Modern Approaches*, 4th edn. Oxford: Blackwell Scientific.

Harrington, R., Whittaker, J., Shoebridge, P. and Campbell, F. (1998). Systematic review of efficacy of cognitive behaviour therapies in childhood and adolescent depressive disorder. *British Medical Journal* 316, 1559–1563.

Hazell, P., O'Connell, D., Heathcote, D. and Henry, D. (2002). Tricyclic drugs for depression in children and adolescents. *Cochrane Database of Systematic Reviews* 2002(2), CD002317.

Healthy Place, America's Mental Health Channel. Available at www.healthyplace. com/ (accessed 2 August, 2009).

Healy, D. and Whitaker, C. (2003). Antidepressants and suicide: Risk-benefit conundrums. *Journal of Psychiatry and Neuroscience* 28, 331–337.

Jacobson, E. (1946). The effect of disappointment on ego and superego formation in normal and depressive development. *Psychoanalytic Review* 33, 129–147.

—— (1953). Contribution to the metapsychology of cyclothymic depression. In P. Greenacre (ed.) *Affective Disorders*. New York: International Universities Press.

—— (1971). *Depression*. New York: International Universities Press.

Jones, E. (1927). Introductory memoir. In *Selected Papers of Karl Abraham*. London: Hogarth Press.

—— (1953). *Sigmund Freud: Life and Work*, Vol. I. London: Hogarth Press.

—— (1957). *Sigmund Freud: Life and Work*, Vol. III. London: Hogarth Press.

Jureidini, J., Doecke, C., Mansfield, P., Haby, M., Menkes, D. and Tonkin, A. (2004a). Efficacy and safety of antidepressants for children and adolescents. *British Medical Journal* 328: 879–883.

Jureidini, J., Tonkin, A. and Mansfield, P. (2004b). TADS study raises concerns. *British Medical Journal* 329, 1343–1344.

Kierkegaard, S. (1843). *Either/Or: Fragment of a Life, Part 1*. London: Penguin, 1992.

Kirsch, I. (2009). *The Emperor's New Drugs: Exploding the Antidepressant Myth*. London: The Bodley Head.

Kirsch, I., Moore, T. J., Scoboria, A. and Nicholls, S. (2002). The emperor's new drugs: An analysis of antidepressant medication data submitted to the U.S. Food and Drug Administration. *Prevention and Treatment* 5, Article 23.

Kirsch, I., Deacon, B. J., Huedo-Medina, T. B., Scoboria, A., Moore, T. J. and Johnson, B. T. (2008). Initial severity and antidepressant benefits: A meta-analysis of data submitted to the Food and Drug Administration. *PLoS Medicine* 5(2), e45 EP.

Klein, M. (1932). The psychoanalysis of children. In *The Writings of Melanie Klein*, Vol. 2. London: Hogarth Press, 1975.

—— (1935). A contribution to the psychogenesis of manic-depressive states. In *The Writings of Melanie Klein*, Vol. 2. London: Hogarth Press, 1975.

—— (1936). Weaning. In *The Writings of Melanie Klein*, Vol. 1. London: Hogarth Press, 1975.

—— (1940). Mourning and its relation to manic-depressive states. In *The Writings of Melanie Klein*, Vol. 2. London: Hogarth Press, 1975.

—— (1963). On the sense of loneliness. In *The Writings of Melanie Klein*, Vol. 3. London: Hogarth Press, 1975.

Knekt, P., Lindfors. O., Härkänen, T., Välikoski, M., Virtala, E., Laaksonen, M. A. et al. (2008). Randomized trial on the effectiveness of long-and short-term psychodynamic psychotherapy and solution-focused therapy on psychiatric symptoms during a 3-year follow-up. *Psychological Medicine* 38, 689–703.

Kraepelin, E. (1902). *Clinical Psychiatry*. New York: Macmillan.

—— (1921). *Manic-Depressive Insanity and Paranoia*. Edinburgh: E. and G. Livingstone.

Kupfer, D. F., Frank, E., Perel, J. M., Cornes, C., Mallinger, A. G., Thase, M. E. et al. (1992). Five-year outcome for maintenance therapies in recurrent depression. *Archives of General Psychiatry* 49, 767–773.

Kutcher, S. (1997). *Child and Adolescent Psychopharmacology*. Philadelphia, PA: Saunders.

Lacan, J. (1949). The mirror stage. In P. du Gay, J. Evans and P. Redman (eds) *Identity: A Reader*. London: Sage, 2000.

Laplanche, J. (1976). *Life and Death in Psychoanalysis*. Baltimore, MD: Johns Hopkins University Press.

Leichsenring, F. and Rabung, S. (2008). Effectiveness of long-term psychodynamic psychotherapy: A meta-analysis. *Journal of the American Medical Association* 300, 1551–1555.

Lenzer, J. (2004). Journalists on Prozac. *British Medical Journal* 329(7468), 748.

Lewinsohn, P. M., Clarke, G. N., Seeley, J. R. and Rohde, P. (1994). Major depression in community adolescents: Age at onset, episode duration, and time to recurrence. *Journal of the American Academy of Child and Adolescent Psychiatry* 33, 809–818.

Libby, A. M., Orton, H. and Valuck, R. J. (2009). Persisting decline in depression treatment after FDA warnings. *Archives of General Psychiatry* 66(6), 633–639.

McCullough, J. P., Klein, D. N., Keller, M. B., Holzer, C. E., Davis, S. M., Kornstein, S. G. et al. (2000). Comparison of DSM-III-R chronic major depression and major depression superimposed on dysthymia (double depression): Validity of the distinction. *Journal of Abnormal Psychology* 109(3), 419–427.

Martin, A., Young, C., Leckman, J. F., Mukonoweshuro, C., Rosenheck, R. and Leslie, D. (2004). Age effects on antidepressant-induced manic conversion. *Archives of Pediatrics and Adolescent Medicine* 158, 773–780.

Meltzer, D. (1960). Lectures and seminars in Kleinian psychiatry (in collaboration with Esther Bick). In A. Hahn (ed.) *Sincerity and Other Works: Collected Papers of Donald Meltzer*. London: Karnac, 1994.

—— (1963). A contribution to the metapsychology of cyclothymic states. In A. Hahn (ed.) *Sincerity and Other Works: Collected Papers of Donald Meltzer*. London: Karnac, 1994.

—— (1984). *Dream-Life: A Re-examination of the Psychoanalytical Theory and Technique*. Perthshire: Clunie Press.

Michels, R. (2000). Psychoanalysis and its discontents. In P. Brooks and A. Woloch (eds) *Whose Freud? The Place of Psychoanalysis in Contemporary Culture*. New Haven, CT: Yale University Press.

Mulder, R. T. (2002). Personality pathology and treatment outcome in major depression: A review. *American Journal of Psychiatry* 159, 359–371.

Nagera, H. (1970). Children's reactions to the death of important objects. *Psychoanalytic Study of the Child* 25, 360–400.

Newton, P. M. (1995) *Freud: From Youthful Dream to Midlife Crisis*. New York: Guilford Press.

Ogden, T. (2001). Reading Winnicott. *Psychoanalytic Quarterly* 62(2), 299–323.

—— (2003). What's true and whose idea was it? *International Journal of Psychoanalysis* 84(3), 651–606.

Paykel, E. S. (2008). Partial remission, residual symptoms, and relapse in depression. *Dialogues in Clinical Neuroscience* 10(4), 431–437.

PDM Task Force (2006). *Psychodynamic Diagnostic Manual* [PDM]. Silver Spring, MD: Alliance of Psychoanalytic Organizations.

Pedder, J. R. (1982). Failure to mourn, and melancholia. *British Journal of Psychiatry* 141, 329–337.

—— (1987). Some biographical contributions to psychoanalytic theories. *Free Associations* 1K, 10–116.

Peterson, T. (2006). Enhancing the efficacy of antidepressants with psychotherapy. *Journal of Psychopharmacology* 20(3) Supplement, 19–28.

Phillips, T., Salmon, G. and James, A. C. (2003). Prescribing practices in child and adolescent psychiatry: Change over time 1993–2000. *Child and Adolescent Mental Health* 8, 23–28.

Pichon-Rivière, E. (1971). El Processo Grupal. Del Psicoanàlisis a la psicologia social. Buenos Aires: Nueva Vision. Review by Manfredi, S.T. *Rivista di Psicoanalisi* 36, 480–488.

Radó, S. (1928). The problem of melancholia. *International Journal of Psychoanalysis* 9, 420–438.

Reich, W. (1968). Interview with Eissler, K. In M. Higgins and C. M. Raphael (eds) *Reich Speaks of Freud: Wilhelm Reich Discusses his Work and his Relationship with Sigmund Freud*. New York: Farrar, Straus and Giroux, 1968.

Rey, J. H. (1986) The psychodynamics of psychoanalytic and psycholinguistic structures. *Journal of the Melanie Klein Society, 4*. Reprinted in J. H. Rey *Universals of Psychoanalysis in the Treatment of Psychotic and Borderline States*, edited by J. Magagna. London: Free Association Books.

—— (1994a). *Universals of Psychoanalysis in the Treatment of Psychotic and Borderline States*, edited by J. Magagna. London: Free Association Books.

—— (1994b). Further thoughts on that which brings patients to analysis. *British Journal of Psychotherapy* 21(2), 241–256.

Richards, D. A., Hughes-Morley, A., Hayes, R. A., Araya, R., Barkham, M., Bland, J. M. et al. (2009). Collaborative Depression Trial (CADET): Multi-centre randomised controlled trial of collaborative care for depression – study protocol. *BMC Health Services Research 2009* 9, 188.

Roazen, P. (1972). *Freud and his Followers*. London: Penguin.

Roazen, P. and Swerdloff, B. (1995). *Heresy: Sándor Radó and the Psychoanalytic Movement*. Northvale, NJ: Jason Aronson.

Rochlin, G. (1953). The disorder of depression and elation. *Journal of the American Psychoanalytic Association* 1, 438–457.

Rodman, F. R. (2003). *Winnicott: Life and Work*. Cambridge, MA: Perseus.

Rosenbluth, M., Blatt, S., Kennedy, S. H. and Bagby, R. M. (2005). *Depression and Personality: Conceptual and Clinical Challenges*. Arlington, VA: American Psychiatric Association Publishing.

Rosenfeld, H. (1959). An investigation into the psychoanalytic theory of depression. *International Journal of Psychoanalysis* 40(1), 105–129.

—— (1964). On the psychopathology of narcissism: A clinical approach. In H. Rosenfeld, *Psychotic States*. London: Hogarth Press.

Roth, T. and Fonagy, P. (eds) (2006). *What Works for Whom: A Critical Review of Psychotherapy Research*. London: Guilford Press.

Rubens, R. L. (1998). Fairbairn's theory of depression. In N. Skolnick and D. Scharff (eds) *Fairbairn Then and Now*. New York: Analytic Press.

Rutter, M. and Taylor, E. (eds) (2002). *Child and Adolescent Psychiatry: Modern Approaches*, 4th edn. Oxford: Blackwell Scientific.

Ryan, N. D. (2005). Treatment of depression in children and adolescents. *The Lancet* 366(9489), 933–940.

Sandler, J. and Joffe, W. G. (1965). Notes on childhood depression. *International Journal of Psychoanalysis* 46, 88–96.

Schneck, C. D., Miklowitz, D. J., Miyahara, S., Araga, M., Wisniewski, S., Gyulai, L. et al. (2008). The prospective course of rapid-cycling bipolar disorder: Findings from the STEP–BD. *American Journal of Psychiatry* 165, 370–377.

Schur, M. (1972). *Freud: Living and Dying*. New York: International Universities Press.

Segal, H. (1979). *Klein*. London: Karnac Classics.

—— (1991). *Dream, Phantasy and Art*. London: Tavistock.

Solms, M. (2007). Psychoanalytic Approaches to Depression. Education Day opening address to *8th International Neuro-Psychoanalysis Congress, Psycho-analytic Perspectives on Depression*. AKH Vienna, July 2007.

Solomon, A. (2002). *The Noonday Demon: An Anatomy of Depression*. London: Vintage.

Spitz, R. (1946). Anaclytic depression. *Psychoanalytic Study of the Child* 2, 313–342.

Stiles, W. B., Barkham, M., Mellor-Clark, J. and Connell, J. (2008). Effectiveness of cognitive-behavioural, person-centred, and psychodynamic therapies in UK primary-care routine practice: Replication in a larger sample. *Psychological Medicine* 38, 677–688.

Sutherland, J. D. (1985). Bion revisited: Group dynamics and group psychotherapy. In M. Pines (ed.) *Bion and Group Psychotherapy*. London: Tavistock.

Taylor, D. (2008). Psychoanalytic and psychodynamic therapies for depression: The evidence base. *Advances in Psychiatric Treatment* 14, 401–413.

Teasdale, J. D., Segal, Z. V. and Williams, J. M. G. (1995). How does cognitive therapy prevent depressive relapse and why should attentional control (mind-fulness) training help? *Behaviour Research and Therapy* 33, 25–39.

Thornton, E. M. (1984). *The Freudian Fallacy: An Alternative View of Freudian Theory*. Garden City, NY: Dial Press.

Timimi, S. (2004). Rethinking childhood depression. *British Medical Journal* 329, 1394–1396.

—— (2007). Should young people be given antidepressants? No. *British Medical Journal* 335, 751.

United Kingdom NHS NICE (National Institute for Health and Clinical Excellence) (2005). Guidelines on Depression in Children and Young People, September 2005.

United Kingdom NHS NICE (National Institute for Health and Clinical Excellence) (2009). Press Release on Updated Guidance on the Treatment and Management of Depression, October 2009.

Weiss, E. (1944). Clinical aspects of depression. *Psychoanalytic Quarterly* 13, 445–461.

Westen, D., Heim, A. K., Morrison, K., Patterson, M. and Campbell, L. (2002). Simplifying diagnosis using a prototype matching approach: Implications for the next edition of the DSM. In L. E. Beutler and M. L. Malik (eds) *Rethinking the DSM: A Psychological Perspective*. Washington, DC: American Psychological Association.

Whittington, C. J., Kendall, T., Fonagy, P., Cottrell, D., Cotgrove, A. and Boddington, E. (2004). Selective serotonin reuptake inhibitors in childhood depression: Systematic review of published versus unpublished data. *The Lancet* 363(9418), 1341–1345.

Whybrow, P. C. and Mendels, J. (1969). Toward a biology of depression: Some suggestions from neurophysiology. *American Journal of Psychiatry* 125(45), 1491–1500.

Winnicott, D. W. (1935). The manic defence. In D. W. Winnicott, *Through Paediatrics to Psycho-Analysis*. London: Hogarth Press and the Institute of Psychoanalysis, 1975.

—— (1948). Paediatrics and psychiatry. In D. W. Winnicott, *Through Paediatrics to Psycho-Analysis*. London: Hogarth Press and the Institute of Psychoanalysis, 1975.

—— (1954). The depressive position in normal emotional development. In D. W. Winnicott, *Through Paediatrics to Psycho-Analysis*. London: Hogarth Press and the Institute of Psychoanalysis, 1975.

—— (1960). Ego distortions in terms of True or False self. In D. W. Winnicott (ed.) *The Maturational Processes and the Facilitating Environment*. New York: International Universities Press, 1965.

—— (1963). Casework and mental illness. In D. W. Winnicott (ed.) *The Maturational Processes and the Facilitating Environment*. New York: International Universities Press, 1965.

—— (1969). Development of the theme of the mother's unconscious in psychoanalytic practice. In C. Winnicott, R. Shepherd and M. Davis (eds) *D. W. Winnicott: Psychoanalytic Explorations*. London: Karnac, 1989.

—— (1975). *Through Paediatrics to Psycho-Analysis*. London: Hogarth Press and the Institute of Psychoanalysis.

—— (1988). *Human Nature*. London: Free Association Books; New York: Schocken.

—— (1989). Fear of breakdown. In C. Winnicott, R. Shepherd and M. Davis (eds) *D. W. Winnicott: Psychoanalytic Explorations*. London: Karnac.

World Health Organization (WHO) (2001). *The World Health Report 2001: Mental Health: New Understanding, New Hope*. Geneva: World Health Organization.

World Health Organization (n.d.). *Depression Fact Sheet*. Available at www.who.int/mental_health/management/depression/definition/en/ (accessed November 2009).

Zetzel, E. R. (1953). The depressive position. In P. Greenacre (ed.) *Affective Disorders*. New York: International Universities Press.

—— (1960). Introduction: Symposium on 'Depressive Illness'. *International Journal of Psychoanalysis* 41(4–5), 476–480.

Index

Abraham, H. C. 10, 19, 26, 28–9, 36, 59–60, 66, 107; and Freud 20–2, 102; and Klein 22, 23–4, 33, 108, 114, 116; mania 21–2, 23, 41, 59–60; theory of depression 20–4

Adler, A. 107

adolescent depression 62–3

aggressiveness/aggression: aggressive drive (Freud) 11; aggressive energy of the superego 19; melancholic's dynamics of self-infliction 52; and narcissism 28; as starting point of depression 57, 58(Fig.)

ambivalence: ambivalent conflict leading to mania 21–2; and Bion's depression 127–8; conflict with guilt 31–3; and the depressive position depression 31–3, 53; and the melancholic's dynamics of self-infliction 52; and neurotic anxiety 80–1; towards the lost object 37

anaclytic depression 56

anal phase relations/tendencies 21; libidinal aspects of 22

anhedonia 15, 32, 53, 80, 84

antidepressant therapy 1, 2, 7, 8 (*see also* SSRIs); considering the alternatives 87–90; and the depressed child 84–95; doctors' responses to criticisms of 93–5; relapse following termination of 2; risk–benefit analysis 90–3; the scandal of SSRIs 86–7

anxiety: death anxiety 27; depressive 30, 42, 54; hypochondriacal 31, 37, 45; indivisible from depression 33–4, 54; neurotic 80–1; over loss of object's love 31; panic attacks 28, 31;

paranoid 30, 53; and paranoid-schizoid depression (Klein) 29; persecutory 28, 29–30, 53; phantasy and 12; primitive 26

Anzieu, D. 97, 98, 106

apathy 20, 28, 80

Aropax *see* Paroxetine

Axis II personality disorders 5

BDP (brief dynamic psychotherapy) 2, 7

Berlin Society 23

Bernays, Martha 98

Bibring, E. 34, 55

Bion, Betty 126

Bion, Francesca 125

Bion, Julian 125

Bion, Nicola 125

Bion, W. R. 102, 113; containment 44, 121; **experience of depression** 119–28; (bad, mad or sad 126–8); (Great War 121–4); (rejected in love 124–5); (schoolboy misery 119–21); (World War II and death of wife 126); and Klein 113, 125, 127–8; mother guilt 113–14, 121, 122–3

Blatt, S. J. 5–6; et al. 6, 56

Bleandonu, G. 119, 123, 126, 127

Bleichmar, H. 57–8

bodily symptoms in depression 30–1, 35–9; anhedonia 15, 32, 53, 80, 84; Meltzer on organ pain 38–9; mental pain and organ pain 36–8; somatic compliance 39

Bonapart, Mary 105–6

Bowlby, J. 34

Breuer, J. 107